Soloing School: Beginner Lead Gu

Published by **www.fundamental-changes.com**

ISBN: 978-1-911267-93-5

www.fundamental-changes.com

Cover Image Copyright: CanStockPhoto - WitthayaP

Contents

Get the Audio

The audio files for this book are available to download for free from **www.fundamental-changes.com** and the link is in the top right corner of the site. Simply select this book title from the drop-down menu and follow the instructions to get the audio.

We recommend that you download the files directly to your computer, not to your tablet, and extract them there before adding them to your media library. You can then put them on your tablet, iPod or burn them to CD. There is a help PDF on the download page, and we provide technical support via the contact form.

Kindle / eReaders

To get the most out of this book, remember that you can double tap any image to enlarge it. Turn off 'column viewing' and hold your Kindle in landscape mode.

Twitter: @guitar_joseph
Over 7500 fans on Facebook: FundamentalChangesInGuitar
Instagram: FundamentalChanges

For over 250 Free Guitar Lessons with Videos Check Out
www.fundamental-changes.com

Introduction

Have you ever wondered why people play air guitar solos at a party or guitar hero on their gaming console? The answer is simple; It's because playing the guitar is awesome and everyone wants to do it!

When friends mimic guitar parts it is likely they are pretending to play a lead guitar solo. In this book, I will give you the tools to play your first *real* guitar solos so you can wow the people around you with your new found skills.

This book teaches you essential scale shapes, technical exercises, drills, rhythm, licks, and full solos. If you are new to playing lead guitar, I recommend working your way through the book from start to finish. That way you will learn and develop techniques and skills in a logical fashion. If you can already play some lead guitar and are just looking for new ideas, then feel free to dive into any chapter you wish.

The most important thing you can do when starting to play lead guitar is to listen! Before you start any of the material in this book, I want you to listen to ten classic guitar solos. The songs presented here are in a blues/rock genre as that will be the primary focus of this book. Make sure you check out the discography at the back of this book for a larger list of great guitar solos.

- Led Zeppelin – Stairway to Heaven (Jimmy Page)
- The Eagles – Hotel California (Don Felder and Joe Walsh)
- Michael Jackson – Beat It (Eddie Van Halen)
- Pink Floyd – Comfortably Numb (David Gilmour)
- Jimi Hendrix – All Along the Watchtower
- Guns N Roses – Sweet Child O Mine (Slash)
- Chuck Berry – Johnny B Goode
- Queen – Bohemian Rhapsody (Brian May)
- Stevie Ray Vaughan and Double Trouble – Texas Flood
- Derek and The Dominos – Layla (Eric Clapton)

When you are listening to these songs, put headphones on and get rid of any other distractions around you, such as your phone or the TV. Shut your eyes and think about what makes these solos so popular. Start a guitar journal with the title 'listening', and write down everything you like about each of the different solos. You can continually add to this listening list throughout your lead playing career. The more you listen, the better! You can, of course, add your favourite solos from any genre of music, not just from rock and blues, but this is a great starting point.

Once you have listened to the tracks mentioned above and started your guitar listening journal, read the tips mentioned on the next page before diving into the exciting world of guitar soloing.

At the end of the book I have provided sample 'workouts' to help you create a balanced practice regime that combines elements from each chapter. These workouts are divided into 15-minute, 20-minute, 30-minute and 60-minute sessions.

The audio for this book is available from **http://www.fundamental-changes.com/download-audio** so you can hear how I play and *phrase* each example.

Happy Playing!

Simon

Tips

Before you dive into the hundreds of musical examples featured throughout this book, take note of these tips featured here.

Relax

Aim to keep as relaxed as possible in all muscles in your hands and arms. If you feel any tension, make a conscious effort to relax or stop playing take a break and come back to what you were working on later.

Breathing

Keep your breathing regular when you play. Sometimes when people concentrate hard on new material they forget to breathe normally.

Don't Get Discouraged

It takes time to learn to play lead guitar solos so maintain a regular practice regime for optimal results.

Short Fingernails

Keep your fingernails short. This will stop any complications from a nail getting in the way of fretting a note.

Sitting Down

At first, I highly recommend sitting down to practice all the material featured in this book. Once you feel comfortable playing the examples you can experiment by standing up. If you are rehearsing for a gig or a live performance make sure you practice the pieces you are working on standing up as well as sitting down. This may sound basic advice, but it can feel strange to play standing up, especially if the first time you stand up while playing guitar is on stage!

Alternate Pick

In general, stick to using alternate picking throughout the examples in this book. Whenever you play a note with a down-pick, the next note should be picked using an up-pick, and vice versa.

Metronome

When you are learning the examples in this book, always use a metronome.

Begin playing each example very slowly with the metronome set at 50bpm and make sure that every note is clean and audible.

Watch your picking hand and notice if you are applying the strict 'down, up' alternate picking pattern required. When you can play an example perfectly three times in a row at 50bpm, raise the metronome up to 53bpm. Continue to increase the metronome speed in increments of 3 beats-per-minute up to your target speed of 80bpm and beyond.

This form of structured practice means that you will only increase your speed once the example is played accurately.

I use the *Tempo* app (by *Frozen Ape*) on my phone as I know I will always have my phone with me, so I never have an excuse to practice without a metronome.

Pain

Stop if you feel any pain. When it comes to guitar playing, 'no pain no gain' is never the way forward. Stretch thoroughly before you play the examples in this chapter and stop if you feel any strain.

Have fun

The most important tip I can give you when playing music is to have fun. Play with other musicians, backing tracks, drum tracks, YouTube videos and enjoy every minute of playing this incredible instrument.

If there is any notation you don't understand, listen to the included audio examples and try to play along with the recorded versions.

Chapter One – The A Minor Pentatonic Scale

Backing Tracks: One-Four

Pentatonic scales contain five notes, and they are your ticket to creative, expressive soloing. In this book, you will look at how to use different types of pentatonic scales in blues, rock, jazz, pop and funk music.

The starting point is the Minor Pentatonic scale as it is the 'bread and butter' approach for most modern guitarists. The guitar allows complete freedom of expression and these pentatonic scales form a palette of colours to enhance your art.

The Minor Pentatonic scale is, without a doubt, the most commonly used scale by guitarists. From the playing of Jimi Hendrix to Eric Clapton, and Larry Carlton to Carlos Santana, many of the greatest guitar solos are based around minor pentatonic ideas.

This scale shape is popular because it is accessible, easy to play, and also sounds fantastic! The Minor Pentatonic is at the root of all blues music and therefore is the basis of every genre of modern music that grew from the blues, such as rock, jazz and funk.

The word 'pentatonic' describes the *construction* of the scale. '*Pent*' means five and '*tonic*' means tones. All the scales in this book, therefore, contain five separate tones.

The A Minor Pentatonic scale contains the notes **A C D E** and **G**.

The examples in this chapter are all in the key of A minor, and each one fits perfectly over an A minor chord or a backing track in A minor such as Backing Track One.

In this chapter, I am going to show you how to get the most out of practising a scale shape. I call the following exercises 'ultimate lick builders'. By learning the examples shown in this chapter you will gain dexterity as well as fretboard fluency within the A Minor Pentatonic scale.

The Minor Pentatonic scale shape is an important starting point when learning to play lead guitar. It will act as a basis for almost all the content you will see in rock guitar, so take your time to digest this scale shape.

Example 1a – A Minor Pentatonic scale

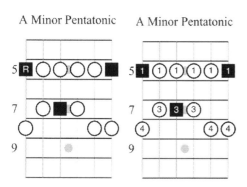

Play the 5th fret of the thickest string (E), with your first finger, then play the 8th fret on that same string with your fourth finger. The next three strings (A, D and G) play frets 5 to 7 using your first and third fingers. On the top strings (B and E) play the 5th and 8th frets with your first and fourth fingers.

Make sure to play this scale shape both ascending and descending using alternate picking (down-pick on the first note and up-pick on the second note of each string.)

Example 1b is identical to the previous example except you pick every note of the A Minor Pentatonic scale twice.

Example 1b –

Next, pick every note of the A Minor Pentatonic scale three times. The rhythm used in this example is called a triplet. Listen to the audio to hear how I play this example.

Example 1c –

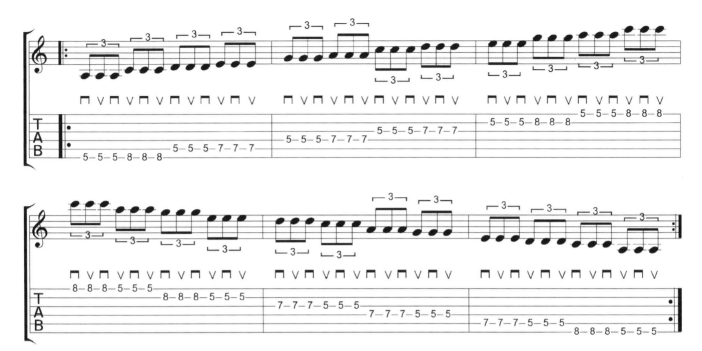

This example shows the A Minor Pentatonic scale with every note being picked four times.

Example 1d –

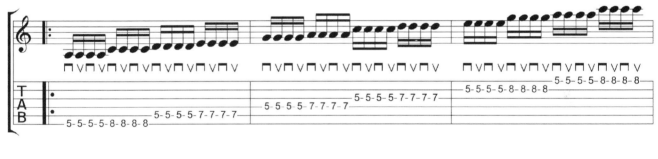

Play through the A Minor Pentatonic scale starting on the highest fret on each string.

Example 1e –

Now work your way back through the A Minor Pentatonic scale shape but start from the lower note on each string.

Example 1f –

The next two examples introduce a string skip. By avoiding playing on adjacent strings, you can add exciting musical jumps into your practice regime.

Example 1g –

Example 1h –

Another way to practice scales is to group them into patterns of three notes. Play the first three notes of the A Minor Pentatonic scale, then start on the second note of the scale and play three ascending notes. Continue this pattern throughout the whole scale shape.

Example 1i –

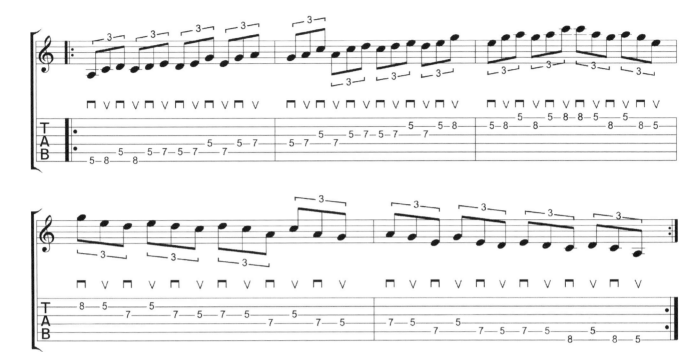

Example 1j –

Now group the A Minor Pentatonic scale into a pattern of four notes.

Example 1k demonstrates playing the scale using a grouping of six notes. This is a common rock guitar pattern used by guitarists like Zakk Wylde.

Example 1k –

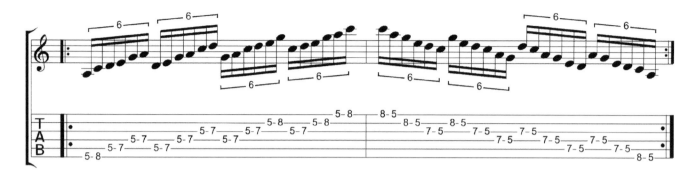

You can create an exciting technical exercise by adding musical jumps. This helps break away from predictable scale runs.

Example 1l –

The exercises in this chapter will make all the following musical ideas easier. Training your fingers to learn a scale shape off by heart does require some work, but you will reap the benefits when you no longer have to think about the scale shape you are playing when soloing.

Practice these scale exercises with a metronome very slowly (around 50 beats per minute) and only raise the tempo when you can play an example perfectly three times in a row.

Chapter Two – Building Melodies

Backing Tracks One to Four.

This chapter shows you how to build your own solos from short fragments of melody. All examples in this section are created using the A Minor Pentatonic scale. These melodic building blocks can act as the stepping stone to creating longer licks and eventually solos. Make sure you play these examples along with backing tracks one to four.

Example 2a uses the notes A and G with a simple rhythmic pattern to create a bite-sized A Minor Pentatonic phrase.

Example 2a –

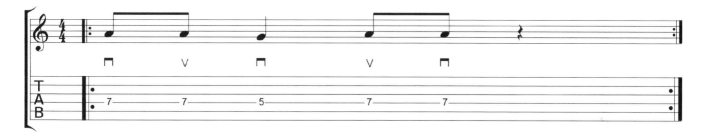

Example 2b uses the same rhythmic pattern but uses the frets on the A string.

Example 2b –

Now combine the previous two examples to create this two-bar motif.

Example 2c –

Example 2d is a typical Minor Pentatonic pattern that occurs a lot in blues and rock guitar playing. Make sure you listen to the attached audio files to see how I phrase every example.

Example 2d –

Next, repeat the pattern in the previous example but now start the pattern from the A string.

Example 2e –

By combining example 2d and 2e, you can create a two-bar phrase.

Example 2f –

Example 2g demonstrates a simple melodic line using the higher pitched notes of the A Minor Pentatonic scale.

Example 2g –

Before playing each example make sure you listen to the accompanying audio tracks available to download from **www.fundamental-changes.com**

Example 2h –

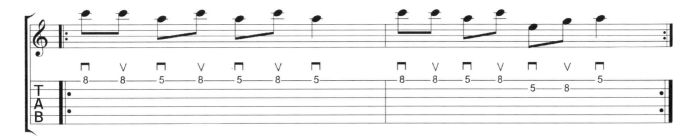

Melodic phrases can be easily combined to create longer licks and solos. Example 2i shows this by combining the previous examples to create a four-bar Minor Pentatonic phrase. This example is a fun one to play over backing track one.

Example 2i –

Mini Solos

The next examples are written to compliment different A Minor backing tracks. These examples introduce the concept that you do not have to play on every beat of the bar, in fact, leaving space is one of the most important things in music. As Mozart once said, "The music is not in the notes, but in the silence between". Listen to how I phrase every example then practice each one along with the backing tracks or metronome.

Examples 2j and 2k should be played over Backing Track One.

Example 2j –

Example 2k –

Use Backing Track Two for example 2l.

Example 2l -

Example 2m shows that sometimes you can leave a large amount of silence at the start of a solo before creating a big impact later in bar one. Play this example with Backing Track One.

Example 2m –

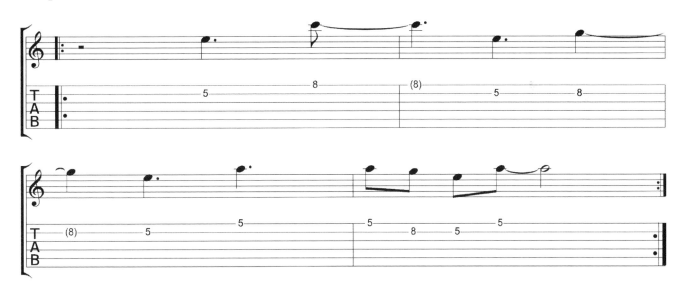

Here is the same melody line is written in a lower octave. Once again use Backing Track One for this example.

Example 2n –

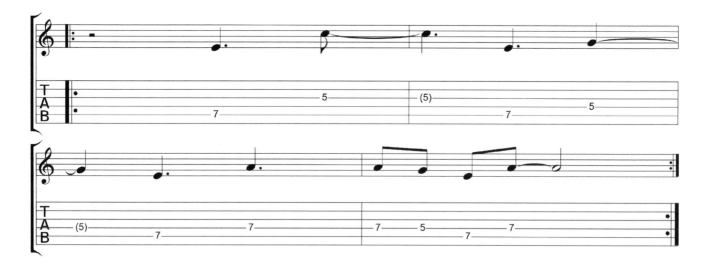

By combining the previous two examples, an eight-bar solo fragment can be created.

Example 2o –

Pop Quiz

What are the notes in the A Minor Pentatonic Scale?

What is the point of learning melodic building blocks?

How many of the examples featured in this chapter can you play without reading them?

Answers on page **105**

Chapter Three – Slides

The concept of a slide is simple: Fret a note on any string, pick it, and then slide your finger to another note on the same string without re-picking. There are only two types of slides, an upward slide (from a lower pitch to a higher one), and a downward slide (from a higher pitch to a lower one).

Slides are particularly common in blues and rock guitar playing but can be found in almost any genre including country, jazz and funk.

The following examples use the A Minor Pentatonic scale.

The aim when learning to slide is to feel comfortable sliding on any finger. However, at first, just use your first finger when you learn these examples. After you have completed each exercise on your first finger, move onto your second, third and fourth fingers.

Upward Slide

Example 3a –

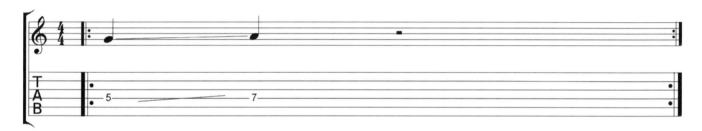

You may have found that after you picked the first pitch that the note 'died' as you tried to slide it up to the 7th fret. The crucial thing when sliding is to apply continuous pressure to the string to keep the note ringing.

Repeat example 3a but apply consistent pressure to the note as you slide it upwards.

In example 3b, play four slides in one bar, back to back. If you want an extra challenge, alternate which finger plays each slide.

Example 3b –

Downward Slide

Example 3c demonstrates the downward slide. Start on the 7th fret and slide down to the 5th fret. Once again apply continuous pressure throughout the slide.

Example 3c –

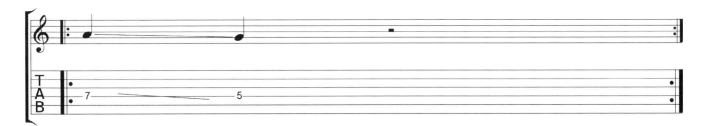

Now play four downward slides within one bar.

Example 3d –

Double Slides

Example 3e introduces a *double slide*. This time slide from the 5th fret to the 7th fret and back to the 5th fret again, all with one pick stroke. It is crucial to keep the pressure on the string while sliding. Aim to slide into the middle of the fret to avoid unwanted buzzes and muting.

Example 3e –

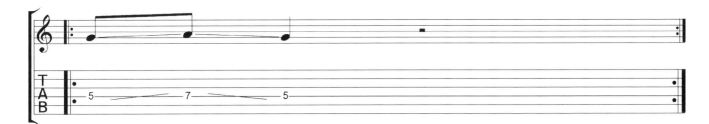

All of the slide examples featured in this chapter are as building blocks for future Minor Pentatonic licks.

Example 3f –

Changing String

Next, move onto the B string and slide from the 5th fret to the 8th fret.

Example 3g –

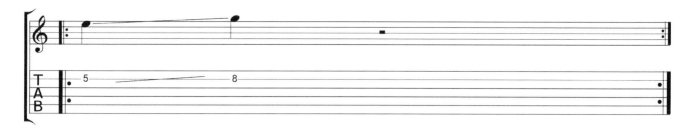

Now slide the 5th fret to the 8th fret four times in one bar.

Example 3h –

Play a downward slide from the 8th fret to the 5th fret to complete example 3i.

Example 3i –

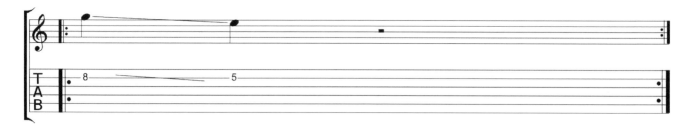

Don't forget to play along to any of the A Minor backing tracks with the examples featured here.

Example 3j –

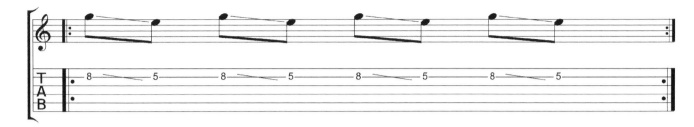

Now apply a double slide (up and down) on the B string between the 5th and 8th frets.

Example 3k –

Example 3l demonstrates two double slides within one bar.

Example 3l –

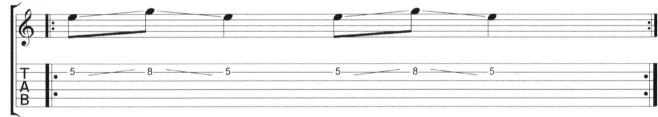

Fundamental Slide Licks

Now that you have got the idea of slides is and how they are created, it is time to put them into a practical soloing context by creating licks with the A Minor Pentatonic scale.

Start the first example with your third finger and slide between the 5th and 7th frets of the A string. That way you will have fingers in the right place to play the rest of this blues lick.

Example 3m –

Once again, start with your third finger to complete the 5th to the 7th fret slide on the D string. You can also play the final double slide on your third finger too. If it feels uncomfortable to slide on your third finger, go back to the start of this chapter and complete the earlier examples on all fingers before attempting these slide licks.

Example 3n –

You can complete example 3o by playing all the slides with your first finger, but experiment by playing the slides on different fingers to see which combination feels most comfortable to you.

Example 3o –

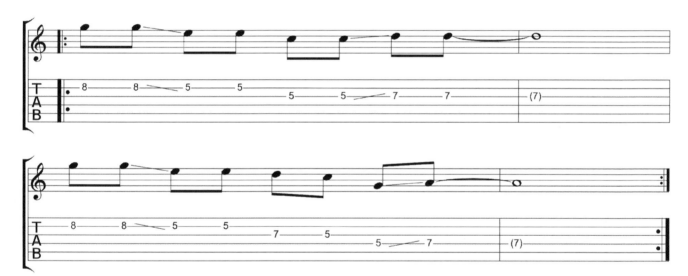

Pop Quiz

How many types of slide are there?

What is an upward slide?

What is a double slide?

What genres of guitar playing might you hear slides being played?

Answers on page **105**

Chapter Four – Bends

Bending is the technique of raising the pitch of a note by increasing the tension on the string. String bending produces a smooth, expressive sound and gives a 'vocal' quality to your solos. By bending a string, you can create one, or several new pitches without picking any other notes. Many famous rock guitarists including David Gilmour, Jimi Hendrix and Carlos Santana are all instantly recognisable by their unique approach to string bending.

The idea of a bend is normally to raise the pitch of a fretted note by a set amount. For example, you may wish to bend the string up by a tone (whole-step), or up by a semitone (half-step). Making sure the bend is accurate and in tune is the priority when learning to bend strings. Developing both the strength needed to bend the string and the aural skill to hear when the bent note is played in tune requires dedicated practice. The following examples will teach how to bend perfectly in tune.

Consider your string gauge before attempting the exercises in this chapter. It is more difficult to bend thicker (heavier) gauge strings, despite the improved tone they produce. The audio examples were recorded using Ernie Ball Super Slinkys (gauge 9-42).

The semitone (one-fret) bend is a common bend, especially in Blues and Rock guitar. In the example 4a, the 8th fret of the G string acts as the target pitch when bending up from the 7th fret.

Example 4a –

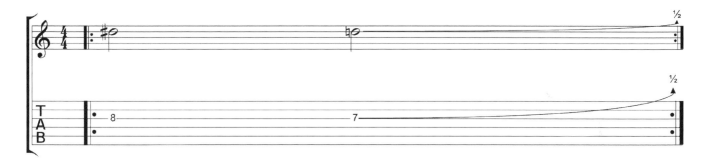

Now bend the 7th fret on the G string up a semitone without using the 8th fret as a target pitch.

Example 4b –

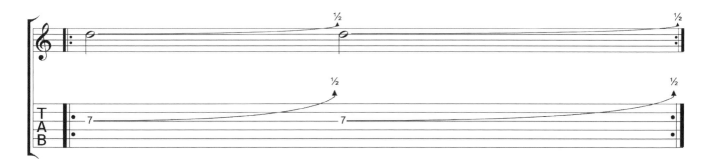

Example 4c demonstrates playing four semitone bends within one bar.

Example 4c –

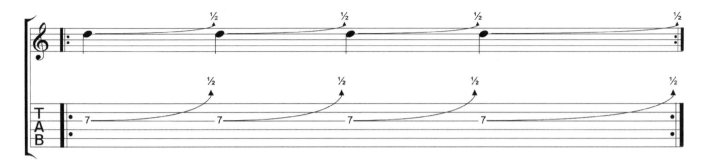

The whole-tone bend (two-frets) is the most common bend in modern electric guitar playing.

In example 4d, play the 9th fret of the G string as a reference or 'target' note before bending the 7th fret of the same string upwards until you have replicated the original 9th fret pitch.

Play the 7th fret note with your third finger and place fingers one and two on the same string (behind the fretting finger) to provide strength and support. Always support any bend with spare fingers whenever possible. This bend will require slightly more force than the previous examples.

Example 4d –

Next, bend the 7th fret a tone without using the 9th fret as your target pitch.

Example 4e –

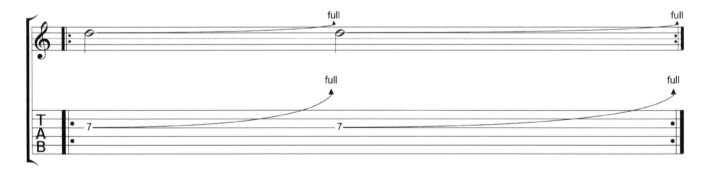

Play four, whole-tone bends in one bar in example 4f, one on each beat.

Example 4f –

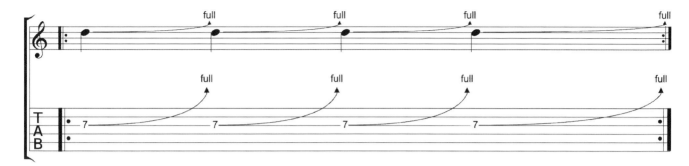

Now that you can play semitone and whole-tone bends on the G string, it is time to explore another common place to use a bend within the A Minor Pentatonic scale. Play the 10th fret of the B string as your target pitch and then bend the 8th fret until it matches that pitch exactly.

Example 4g –

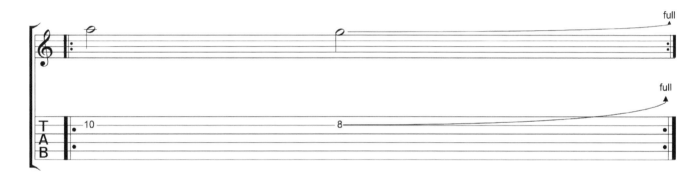

Practice playing a whole-tone bend on the B string *without* using the 10th fret as a target pitch.

Example 4h –

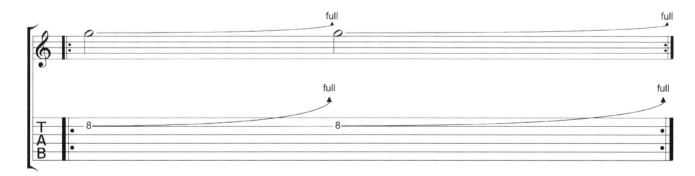

Play four, whole-tone bends on the B string, one on every beat of the bar.

Example 4i –

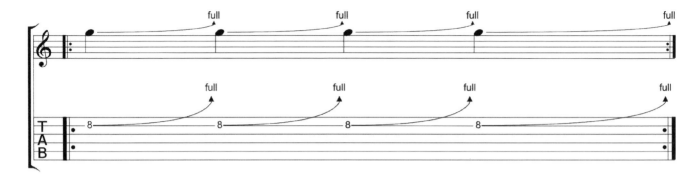

The final set of bends in this chapter use the high E string. Keeping to the A Minor Pentatonic scale, these bends are based around the 8th fret.

Example 4j uses the 10th fret as a target pitch before bending the 8th fret to match.

Example 4j –

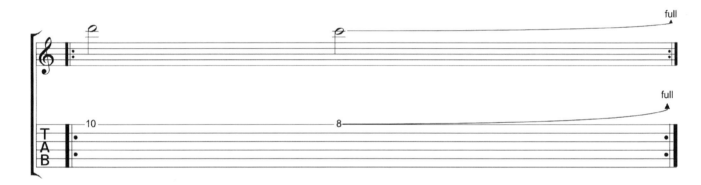

Bend the 8th fret up a tone without playing a target pitch note first.

Example 4k –

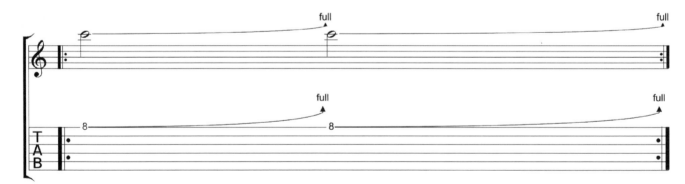

Four, whole-tone bends on the high E string make up example 4l. Make sure you download the audio for this book and listen to every example before playing it yourself.

Example 4l –

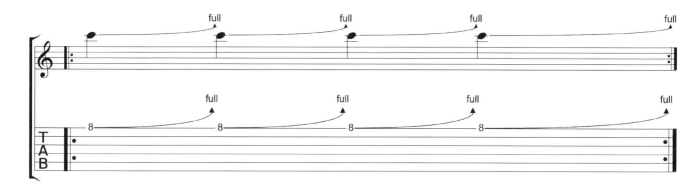

Core Bending Licks

Once you have mastered how to play a semitone bend and a tone bend in multiple places you can move onto building blues-rock licks that use the A Minor Pentatonic scale. Play these along with Backing Tracks One – Four.

Bend the 7th fret of the G string and hold that bend for two beats before playing the 5th fret of the G string, then resolving to the 7th fret of the D string.

Bends Around the G String

Example 4m –

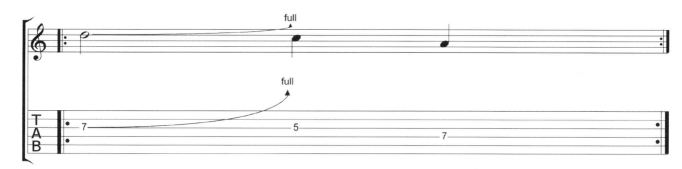

The tone bend is the most common bend in modern day guitar playing so if this still feels uncomfortable don't worry, just go back to practising it on its own before applying it to the licks written here.

Example 4n –

It is more important to internalise and remember these licks than it is to read them off the page. As you go through this chapter pick your favourites and spend extra time learning them.

Example 4o –

Example 4p –

As well as learning the above examples, I encourage you to experiment by creating your own ideas. Use these patterns as a basis, but change the order you play the notes. For example, you could play a phrase backwards by starting at the end of a bar.

Example 4p –

The last few examples have focussed around the tone bend on the 7th fret of the G string. The next examples focus around the tone bend at the 8th fret of the B string.

Bends Around the B String

Example 4q –

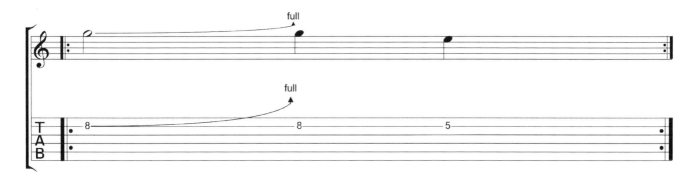

Example 4r –

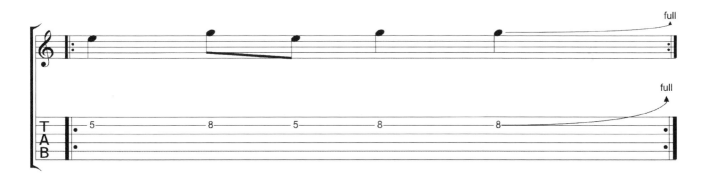

Example 4s –

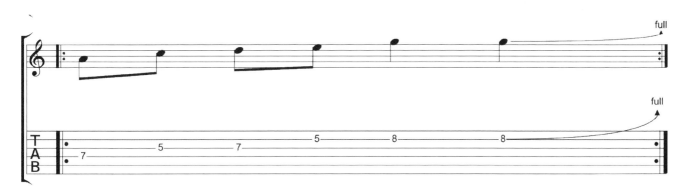

Now you can focus on building some core bending vocabulary around the tone bend on the 8th fret of the high E string.

Bends Around the E String

Example 4t –

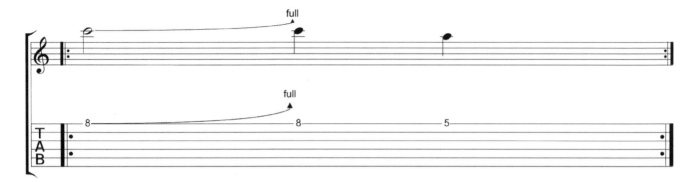

Example 4u –

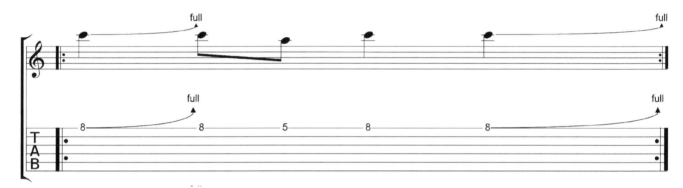

Example 4v –

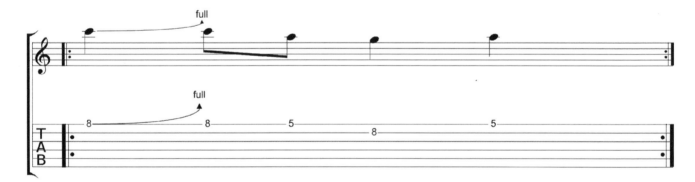

Licks with Multiple Bends

Using one bend in a lick is great, but for maximum impact you can use bends on different strings within one lick. The following examples show how you can build bending licks using the A Minor Pentatonic scale with bends on different strings.

Example 4w –

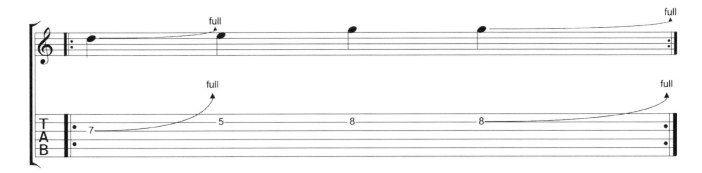

Example 4x –

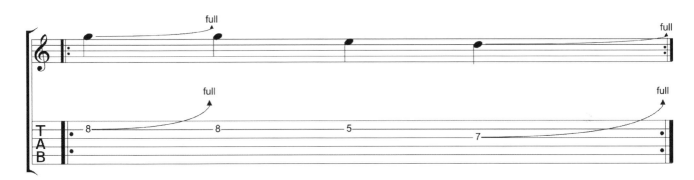

Example 4y –

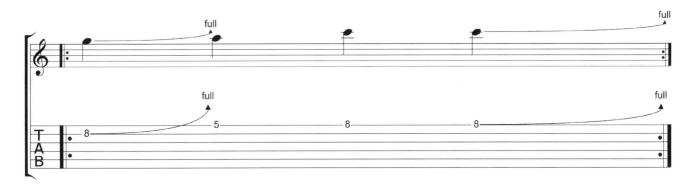

Example 4z –

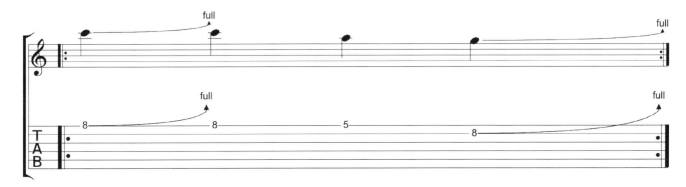

Pop Quiz

What is bending?

What is a semi-tone bend?

What is a tone bend?

What is the most common type of bend in modern electric guitar playing?

Name three guitarists who famously use bending in their playing.

Answers on page **105**

Chapter Five – Legato

In the late 1960s and early 1970s, rock guitarists like Jimmy Page and Brian May began to incorporate faster phrases into their solos. These quicker passages were often created by playing *hammer-ons* and *pull-offs*. Together, these two techniques are referred to as *legato* (Italian for 'smooth'). Some classic examples of legato playing are in Led Zeppelin's Stairway to Heaven solo, Queen's I Want It All solo, and the Red Hot Chili Peppers' track, Snow.

To create a hammer-on, play a note and then quickly 'hammer' a different finger onto a higher fret to create two notes from just one pick stroke. A pull-off is the reverse of a hammer-on. Begin by picking a fretted note and then pull your finger off the string (downwards towards the floor) to sound a fretted note *below* the first.

Legato guitar playing is all about smooth, flowing lines, and lends itself perfectly to melodic rock soloing. An important concern when playing legato is to *keep each note the same volume*. This means that the picked note and the legato notes that follow should all have very similar dynamics. Try recording yourself playing the following examples and pay attention to how smooth the transition is between the picked and legato notes.

There are many legato technique-building exercises, and, while useful for developing the fundamental principles, they are often not very musical. The following examples aim to keep each exercise musical while developing great technique. Listen to the audio examples first to hear how these examples should sound before trying them yourself.

Stick to the *one-finger-per-fret* rule when learning these examples unless otherwise stated. The idea behind the rule is that you allocate one finger to each fret that you play. For example, if you are playing notes between the 5th and 8th frets, use your first finger for the 5th fret's notes and your second finger for all 6th fret's notes, etc. This can be seen in the diagram below:

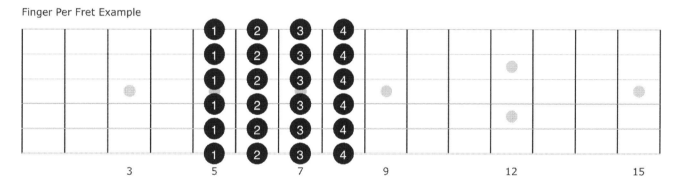

Key points to consider:

1) Ensure there is space between the fingers of your fretting hand when playing legato. By learning to play legato with room between your fingers, you will develop strength in the correct tendons and muscles of the hand.

2) Keep your knuckles upright at all times.

3) Stop if you feel any pain. When it comes to guitar playing, 'no pain no gain' is *never* the way forward. Stretch and warm up thoroughly before you play difficult legato sequences and stop if you feel any strain.

The simplest legato technique is the semitone (one-fret) hammer-on which is demonstrated in the first example. Use your first and second fingers to play this exercise and keep some space between your fingers to help build strength and good technique.

One Fret Hammer On

Example 5a –

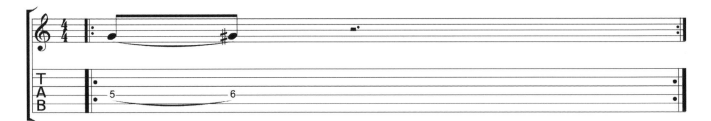

Now play two, one-fret hammer-ons within one bar.

Example 5b –

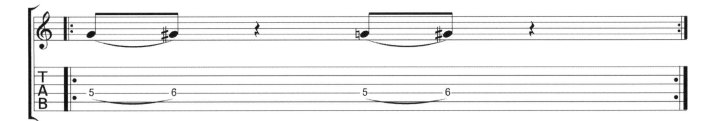

To build up your strength example 5c demonstrates playing four one-fret hammer-ons in one bar.

Example 5c –

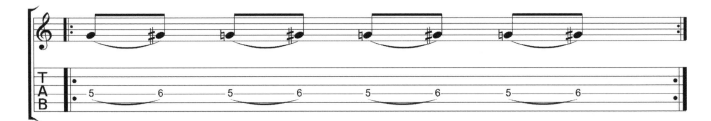

One Fret Pull Off

Example 5d introduces a one-fret pull-off. Remember that you want to hear play notes using just one pick stroke. Place the 5th fret note on the fretboard with your first finger, then play the 6th fret with your second finger. To execute the pull-off, pull your second finger off the string (downwards towards the floor) to sound the 5th fret.

Example 5d –

Now play four, one-fret pull-offs within a bar.

Example 5e –

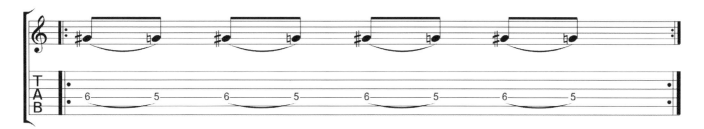

Although one-fret hammer-ons and pull-offs are useful, you will often find that two-fret, or even three-fret legato patterns are more common as they can be applied to many different scale shapes. All the following examples use legato patterns based around A Minor Pentatonic scale.

Example 5f uses a two-fret hammer-on on the D string. Use your first and third fingers to play this pattern.

Example 5f –

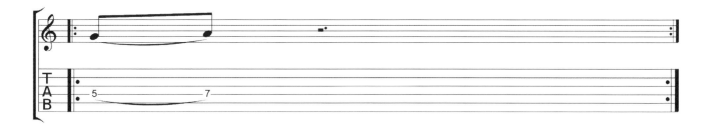

Now play two hammer-ons in one bar.

Example 5g –

For a slightly tougher exercise, play the two-fret hammer-on from the 5th to the 7th frets four times within one bar. If you want to work on stamina and dexterity, be sure to check out my book Guitar Finger Gym.

Example 5h –

Next, play a 7th to 5th fret pull off on the D string.

Example 5i –

Now play two pull-offs within one bar.

Example 5j –

Build up your technique by playing four pull-offs within a one-bar phrase.

Example 5k –

Keeping to the A Minor Pentatonic scale, it is time to examine the three-fret hammer-on and pull-off on the B string. Complete these examples using your first and fourth fingers.

Example 5l –

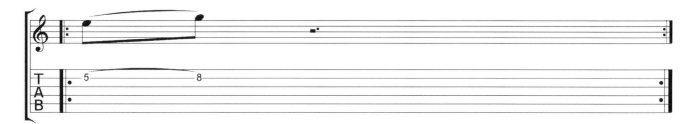

Example 5m –

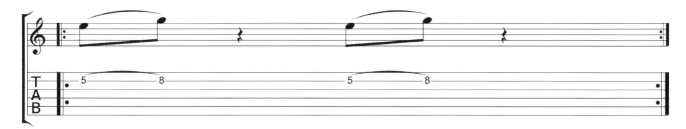

Example 5n –

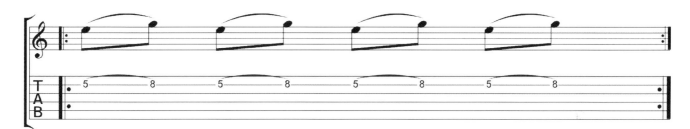

Now work on pulling-off three frets from your fourth finger to your first finger. Practice each example very slowly at around 50bpm before gradually speeding up the metronome when you can complete each example three times in a row.

Example 5o –

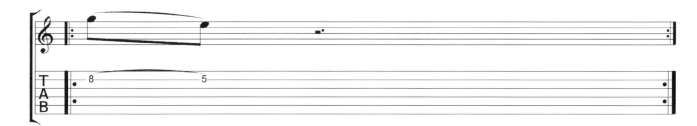

Example 5p –

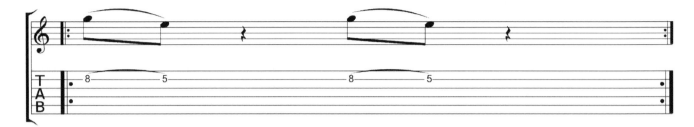

Example 5q –

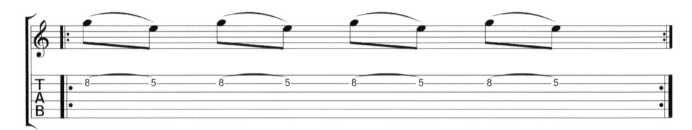

Core Legato Licks

By now it should be apparent that you can use bends and slides around the A Minor Pentatonic scale to create licks. You can also use legato (hammer-ons and pull-offs) to create licks and phrases. Play these licks with backing tracks one - four.

The next examples use hammer-ons to create core blues-rock vocabulary. Listen to the attached audio to see how I play and *phrase* each example.

Example 5r –

Example 5s –

Example 5t –

Now for some pull-off licks.

Example 5u –

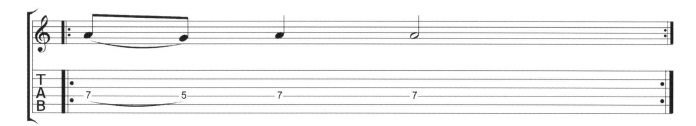

Example 5v –

Example 5w –

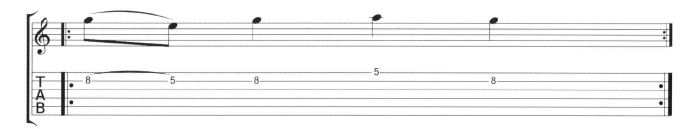

Example 5x –

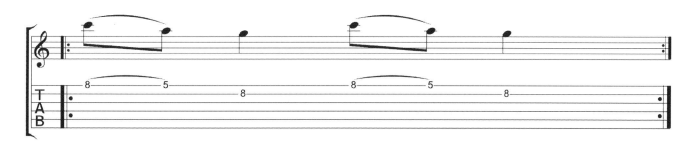

Example 5y –

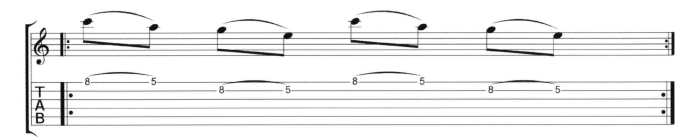

Once you are comfortable combining hammer-ons and pull-offs separately, you can create licks and phrases that combine both of them.

Go through each of these licks and highlight your favourites!

Example 5z –

Example 5z1 –

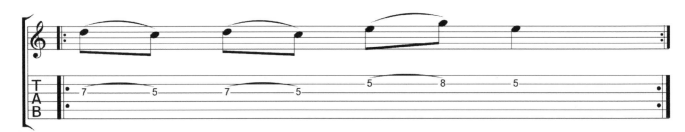

Example 5z2 –

Example 5z3 –

Example 5z4 –

Example 5z5 –

Modern Rock Vibrato

Vibrato adds expression and energy to a note by rapidly moving the pitch up and down. This allows a note to have a more vocal, human quality and gives passion and emotion to your guitar solos. Vibrato is personal and unique to each guitarist and can be added to any note by any finger. It is possible to alter its speed, duration, and the delay before it is added. The amount of vibrato used depends very much on the genre of music, with narrow subtle vibrato often used in the blues, and wide, obvious vibrato more commonly reserved for rock guitar.

Modern rock vibrato is applied by moving the string rapidly in the direction of the fret wire in a similar way to bending a string. This technique gives great control of the pitch variation of a note, and also allows us to add vibrato to a bend. Soft, gentle vibrato suits ballads and slower songs, while wide vibrato works well for harder rock tracks.

If you want a far more in-depth look at vibrato, check out my book **Melodic Rock Soloing for Guitar**.

Example 5z6 (Basic Modern Rock Vibrato Technique)

1. Pick and hold the 7th fret of the G string with your first finger.
2. Place your thumb as if you were going to bend the note.
3. Pull the string down towards the floor using your wrist as a pivot. The vibrato is created by the manipulation of the wrist, rather than the fingers. Release the wrist back to a normal position and let the note return to its original pitch.
4. Repeat this movement as many times as possible (although three times is usually enough in practice).
5. Repeat example 5z6 on each finger. (The fourth finger is used less often, but it is still good practice if you can manage it).

At first, the string might not move very far, but, just as with string bending, it becomes easier with practice.

When you are comfortable with this basic approach, experiment with the amount of vibrato you add and the speed of its manipulation.

The most crucial thing is to ensure that the note doesn't sound out of tune when the vibrato is applied. The more confident you become at using vibrato, the wider the vibrato you can add.

The full concept of how to apply vibrato is quite advanced and is out of the scope of this book but don't worry, if you want a far more in-depth look at vibrato check out my book **Melodic Rock Soloing for Guitar**.

There is a lot of content in this chapter so return here often so you can keep developing your technique.

Take your time and remember there is no rush to complete a chapter; it is not a race! What matters is that you progress consistently over the next few months and years, and that you continuously monitor your development.

Remember that this book, and your guitar playing, should be about enjoyment, so make having fun your priority, and any challenges will feel less significant in comparison.

Chapter Six – A Minor Pentatonic Licks

A guitar *lick* is a short series of notes (or *phrase*) that can be used as the basis for solos and lead guitar playing. Learning licks is like learning vocabulary in a new language. Always remember that music is a language!

In this chapter, I have created nine A Minor Pentatonic licks based on the techniques in the previous chapters. These licks include slides, bends and legato, so make sure you are confident with all these techniques before continuing.

At this point, I want to remind you again to listen to great lead guitar players and immerse yourself in as many different musical genres as possible. Refer to the introduction for ten essential solos, and to the discography at the end of the book for more vital listening.

Example 6a uses a *call and response* blues pattern: Bars one and three are identical and act as the 'call', and bar two and four vary slightly to create the 'response'. This is a fundamental of creating longer phrases by anchoring your solos around one memorable lick throughout.

Example 6a –

In example 6b, I again created a call and response pattern that alternates between a sliding lick in bar one and three and a hammer-on lick in bars two and four. Make sure you listen to the accompanying audio tracks before playing these licks.

Example 6b –

Until now, everything in this book has focussed on playing one note at a time. An excellent way to break up this habit is by using *double-stops* or 'playing two notes simultaneously'. Play the 5th fret notes with your first finger lying across the B and E strings. If you find it difficult to play both frets with just one finger, experiment by using separate fingers.

Chuck Berry uses double-stops a lot in his playing. Check out the classic guitar anthem Johnny B Goode.

Example 6c –

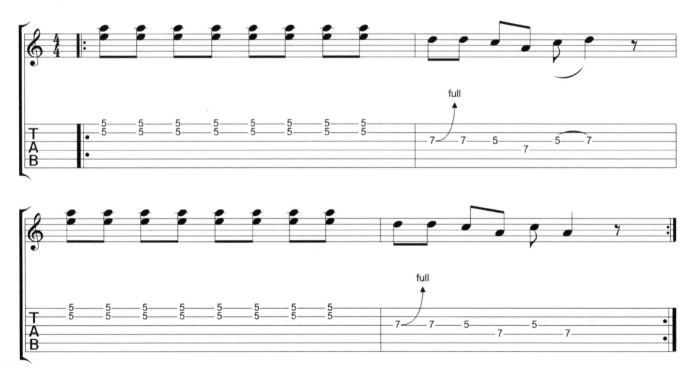

You don't have to play on every beat of the bar!

This tip stuck with me right from my early days of studying at the Guitar Institute. By having audible silence between the notes you play, your licks will sound well-constructed and thought-out.

Remember that 'the plectrum never runs out of breath.' Try singing your licks out loud. Where would the melody naturally pause? Where would you have to breathe? Try to copy this phrasing in your guitar playing.

Example 6d –

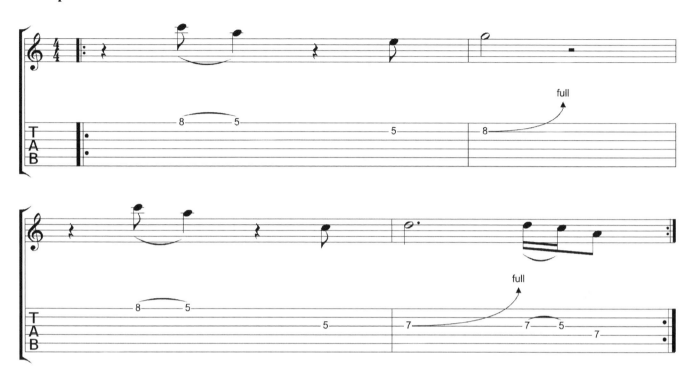

Slide from the 7th fret to the 5th, and back to the 7th fret on the A string using just one pick stroke. This double slide forms the basis of the next lick.

Example 6e –

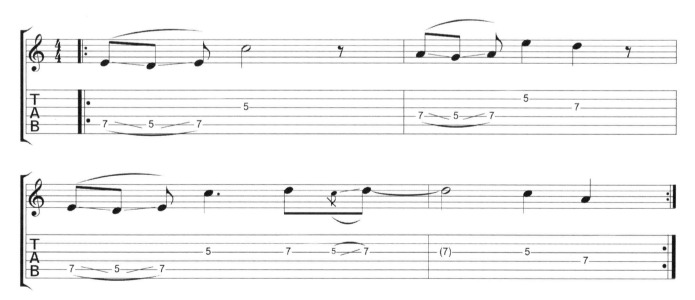

I have created four A Minor backing tracks for you to practice all these licks over. I believe that playing along to backing tracks is one of the most practical and fun ways for you to improve your lead guitar playing skills.

Example 6f –

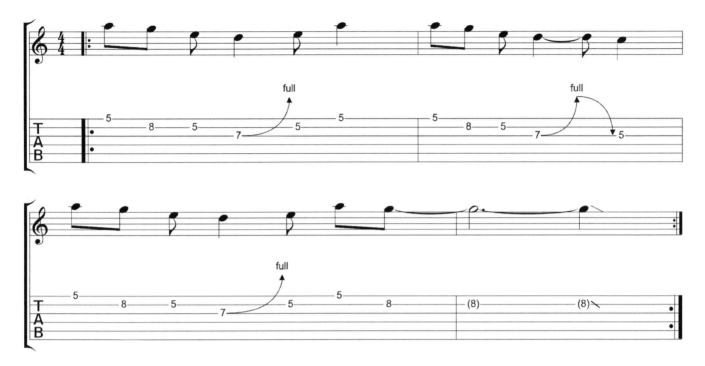

I often sing a melodic phrase first before playing that information on the guitar. This is how example 6g was created.

Example 6g –

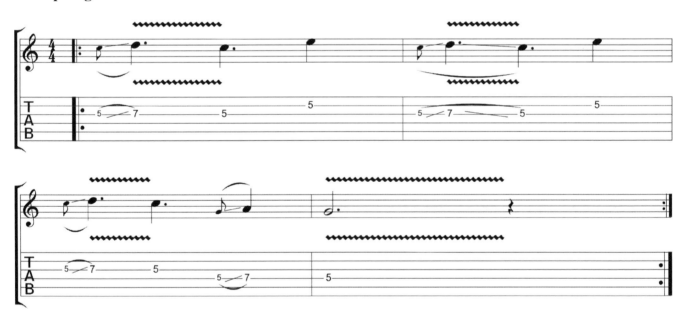

Pull-off patterns are often seen in rock guitar solos. Check out the solo from the Dire Straits hit, Sultans of Swing for more ideas in this style.

Example 6h –

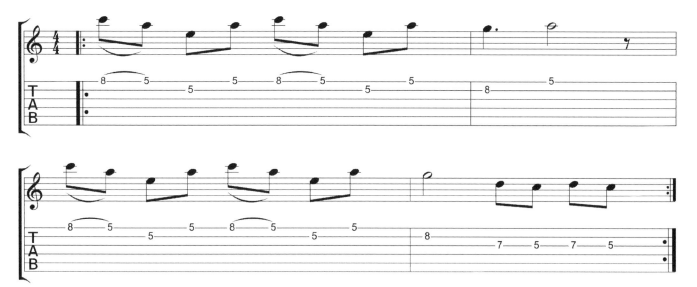

It is important to internalise these licks and not just read them off the page. Play them repeatedly with a backing track or a metronome until you can fret them without the need for the music.

Example 6i –

Now that you have learnt the nine licks, combine these licks in any way you would like. Remember you don't have to use a full lick every time, sometimes just using a few notes from one lick will suffice.

Example 6j –

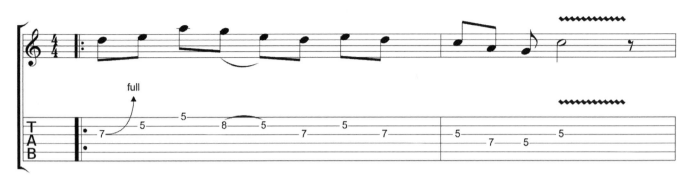

Chapter Seven – A Minor Pentatonic Full Solo

Backing Track One.

There is nothing quite like learning a guitar solo in its entirety to help you internalise and master new techniques. While learning licks and techniques are a solid base for progression on the guitar they won't ever provide the satisfaction that you get from playing along, note-for-note, with a piece of music.

The following solo combines all the techniques and ideas seen throughout this book into a fun, melodic solo. The solo is in the key of A minor and uses the A Minor Pentatonic Scale throughout.

Although, at first, this full solo may seem a little daunting, I have constructed it so that a lot of the licks repeat themselves. The licks featured in this solo are not identical to the licks in the previous chapter but often I have retained similar techniques and phrases so they won't feel completely alien to you.

As well as listening to my performance of this track, I have included a slowed down midi version so you can play along at a slower tempo.

By now you should be very familiar with the A Minor Pentatonic scale shape. One good idea is to learn the notes that the scale contains. In this diagram, you will see the notes of the A Minor Pentatonic scale written out on each string.

A Minor Pentatonic

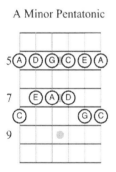

Make sure you have listened to example 7a multiple times in headphones to hear all the expressive phrasing and nuances, and aim to emulate all of them when you play it yourself.

Example 7a – A Minor Pentatonic Full Solo

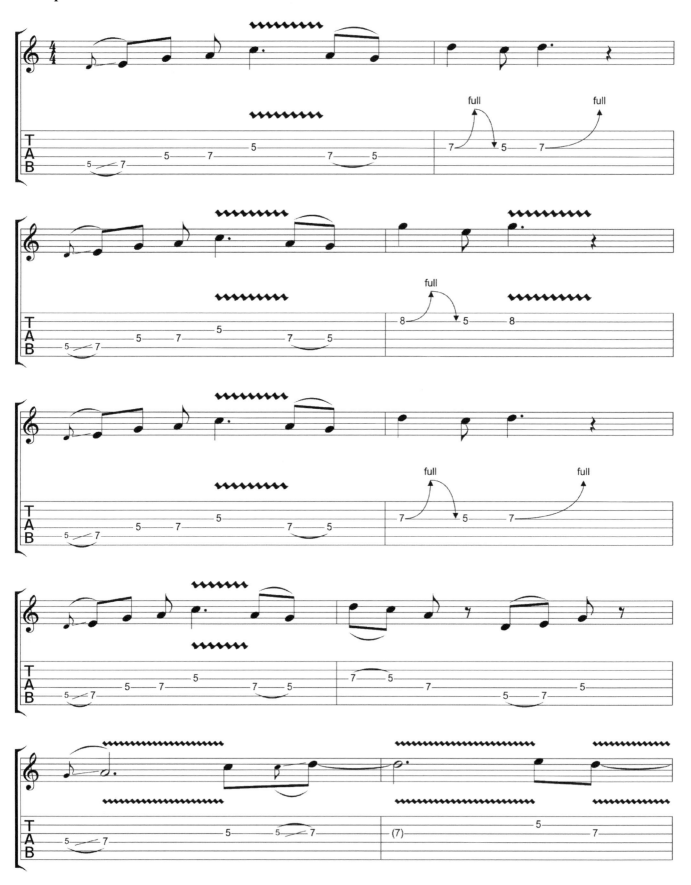

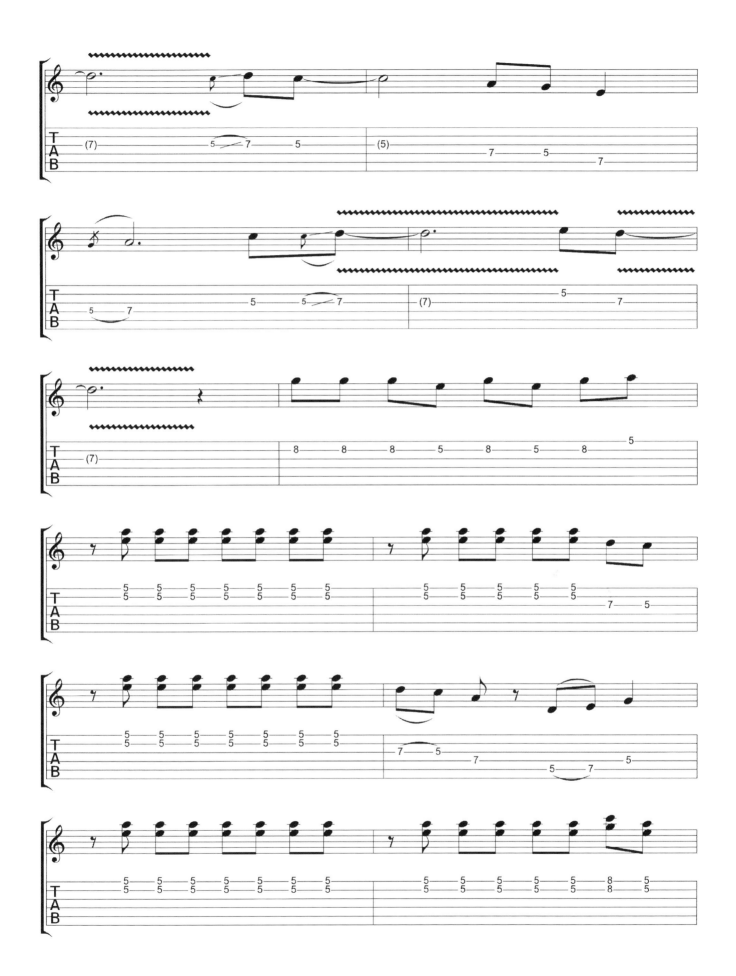

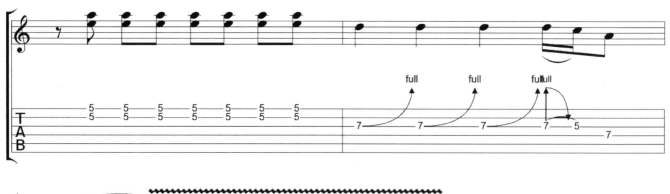

Chapter Eight – Moving to E Minor

Backing Track Five and Six

One of the best things about learning a scale shape on the guitar is that you can easily transfer it to another key by simply moving the scale shape to a different location. I am going to show you how you can move the nine A Minor Pentatonic licks you learnt in Chapter Six up the fretboard into the key of E minor.

Until now, you have learnt the A Minor Pentatonic scale starting from the 5th fret of the 6th string. Let's move that scale shape into the key of E minor by moving the whole shape up to the 12th fret of the 6th string.

Example 8a shows the E Minor Pentatonic scale (E G A B D) starting from the 12th fret of the low E string. Look at the second diagram below to see which finger should be placed in each fret.

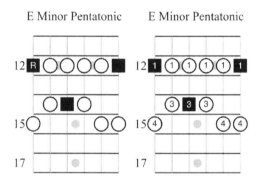

Example 8a –

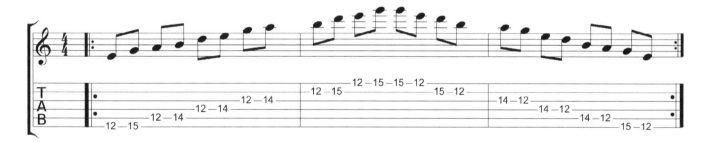

I am a long term believer that everything you do on the guitar should be about maximising the information you already know. The nine licks I have created here are the same as in Chapter Six, but now they are moved up around the 12th fret shape of E Minor Pentatonic. These licks should feel comfortable quite quickly if you have spent time learning them earlier on. Having the ability to move licks into any key will mean you can play solos over a wide variety of tracks.

Example 8a demonstrates a four-bar, call and response blues pattern around the E Minor Pentatonic scale at the 12th fret.

Example 8b –

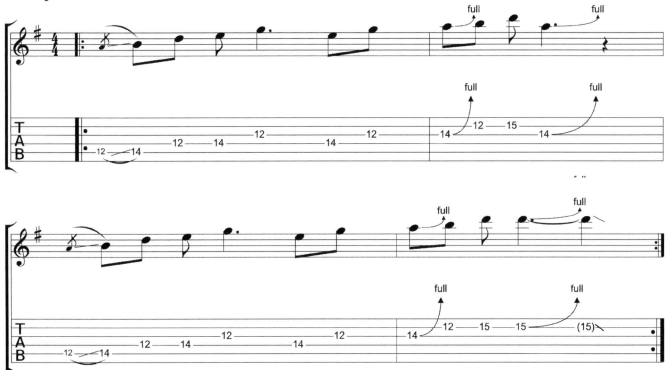

In example 8b I again created a call and response pattern using the E Minor Pentatonic scale. This alternates between a sliding lick in bar one and three, and a hammer-on lick in bars two and four.

Example 8c –

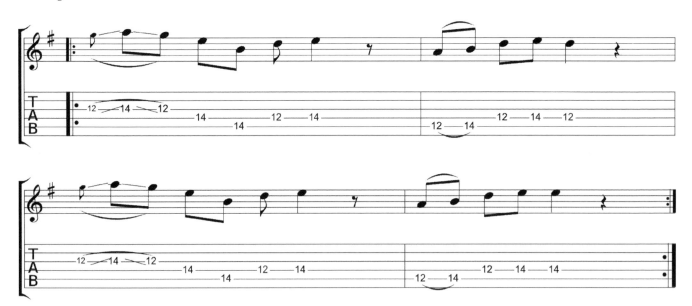

Now for a double-stop lick. Alternating between single-note and double-stop patterns adds a nice variation to your lead guitar sound.

Example 8d –

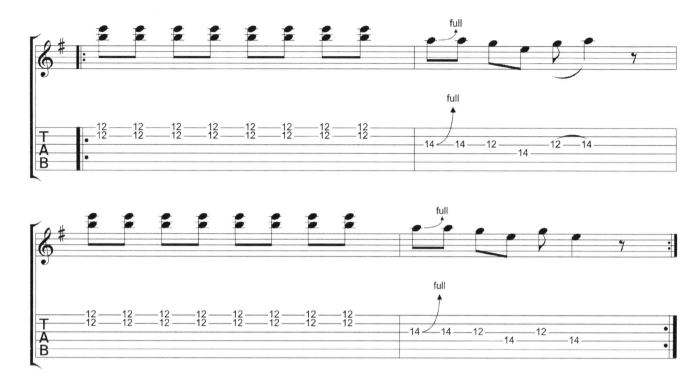

Adding in rests between notes adds a vocal quality to your licks.

Example 8e –

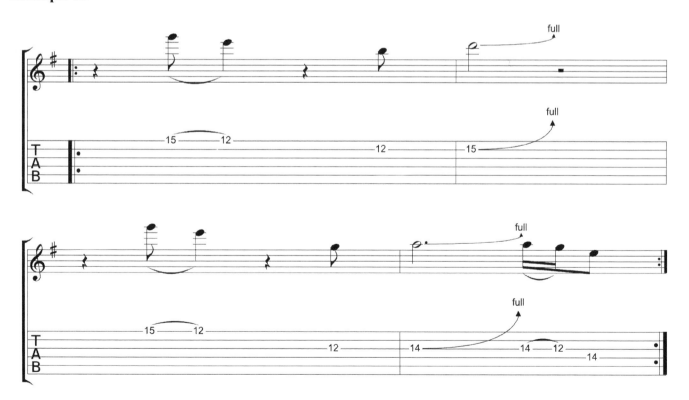

Check out the main melody of Steve Vai's masterpiece, For The Love Of God, for a great example of melodic slide vocabulary.

Example 8f –

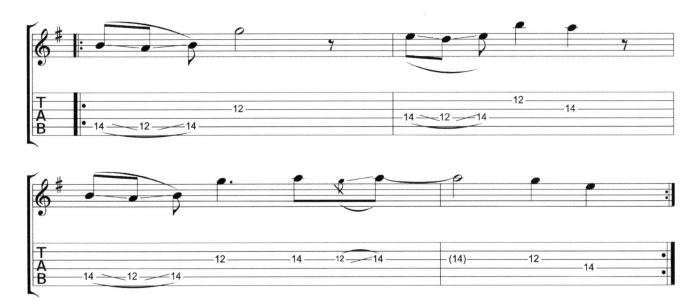

Example 8g is reminiscent of Jimi Hendrix as he often used the E Minor Pentatonic scale in his solos. Check out Hey Joe for an incredible example of this.

Example 8g–

Listen closely to how I play each note with the accompanying audio tracks provided. In example 8h, I add subtle vibrato to each note to add an expressive vocal quality.

Example 8h –

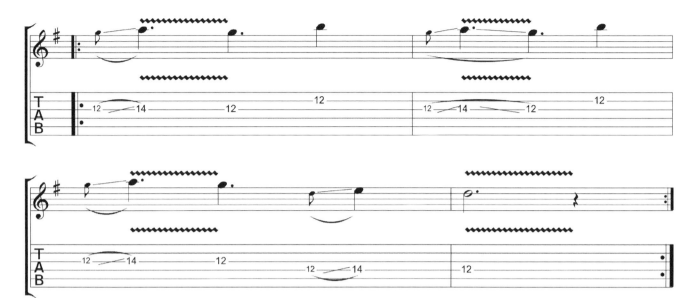

Aim to make your legato lines as fluid as possible by ensuring that the picked notes are the same volume as the hammer-ons/pull-offs.

Example 8i –

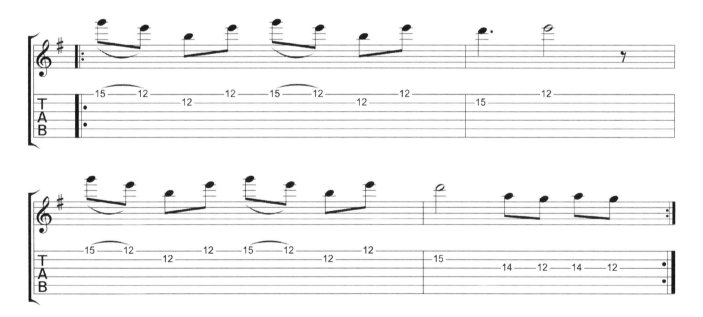

Although you can quite quickly build speed using legato techniques, it is more important that the notes are fretted correctly. Only build up speed when you can play a lick/phrase correctly three times in a row with a metronome.

Example 8j –

Practice your E Minor Pentatonic licks along to backing tracks five and six.

Example 8k –

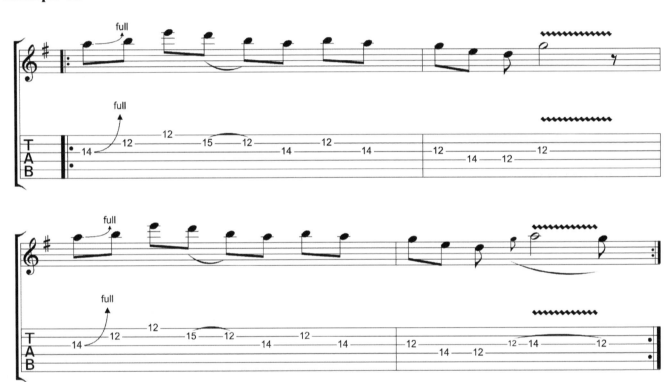

Now that you have learnt the E Minor Pentatonic scale shape and have been able to transfer licks from A Minor to E Minor, it is important to understand how you can move these licks into any key. The diagram below shows the notes on the 6th string. You can play the Minor Pentatonic scale starting from any of these notes on the 6th string. For example, if you start the Minor Pentatonic scale shape from the 7th fret you create B Minor pentatonic. Try moving all the licks from this chapter into a new key.

6th String Notes

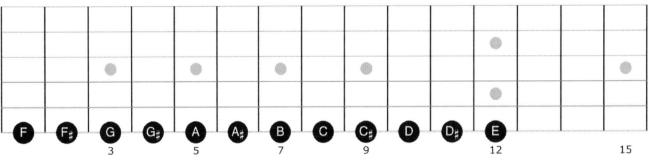

Chapter Nine – E Minor Solo

Backing Track Six.

Example 9a is a full solo that uses the E Minor Pentatonic scale that should be played over the top of Backing Track Six.

All the full solos in this book are constructed so that some of the licks repeat themselves. This helps to develop the theme of the solo and also prevents it from feeling too intimidating to attempt.

This solo uses both single-notes and double-stop patterns. In bar 9, use your first finger to cover both the D, and the G string; that way you will have your third finger free to complete the hammer-on. Remember that you should always aim to use the one-finger-per-fret rule, so if you have more than one note on one fret, use one finger to play both notes.

This solo presents a lot of material and is something you can both learn in full and steal individual licks from. Keep coming back to it over time, and you will find new fragments of lead playing vocabulary had not previously committed to memory.

Put headphones on and listen to example 9a at least three times before you attempt to play it. When your brain has a great idea of what something should sound like, it will help you zone in on the specific expressive techniques you need to play. This applies to learning any new melody, solo, or lead guitar phrase.

As well as my performance of this track, I have included a slowed down midi version so you can play along at a slower tempo.

Example 9a –

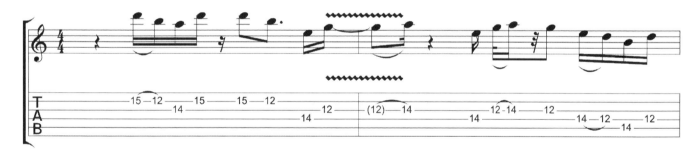

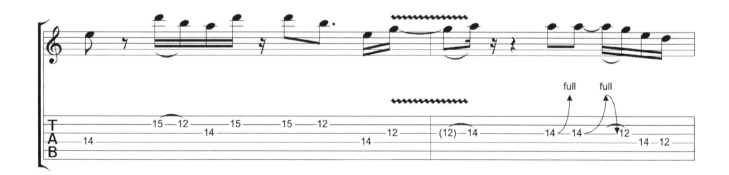

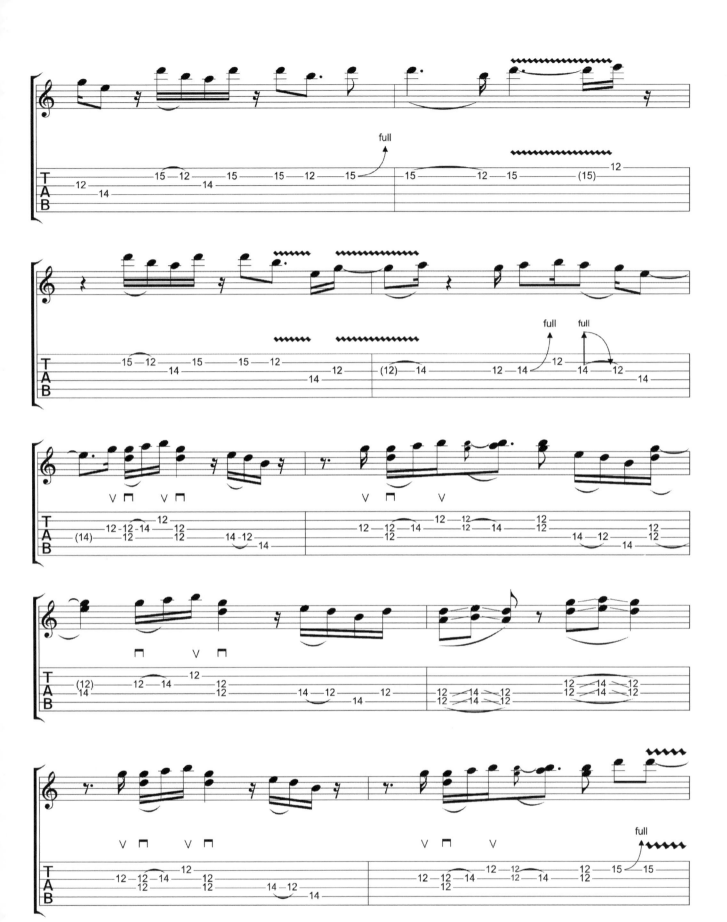

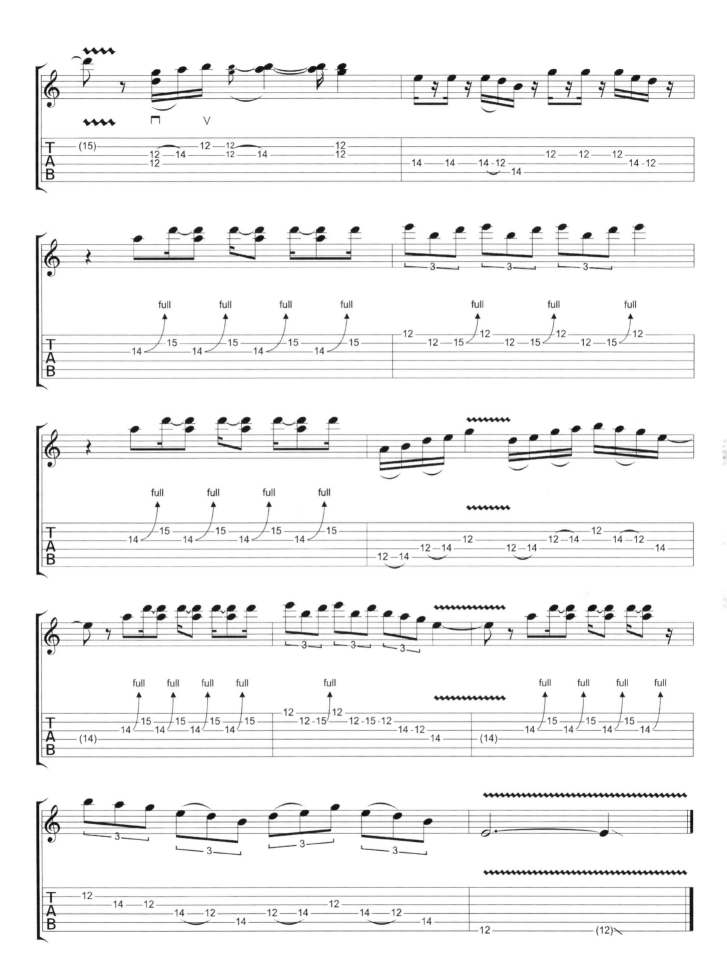

Pop Quiz

What notes are in the E Minor Pentatonic scale?

What is a double-stop?

How can you develop a theme in a solo?

How many times should you listen to a solo with headphones on before attempting to play it?

Answers on page **105**

Chapter Ten – The A Blues Scale

The A Blues scale is identical to the A Minor Pentatonic scale except that it contains one extra note, 'Eb'. The notes in the A Blues scale are **A C D Eb E G**.

The Blues scale is enormously popular among electric guitar players and is often used by guitarists like Angus Young and Joe Satriani.

The examples in this chapter are all in the key of A minor, and each lick fits perfectly over an A minor chord or a backing track in A minor such as Backing Track One.

By learning the examples shown in this chapter you will gain dexterity as well as fretboard fluency within the A Blues scale.

You can play The A Blues scale in the following way on the guitar:

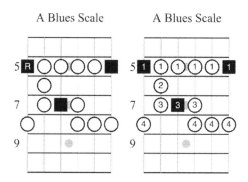

Ascend and descend the A Blues scale in example 10a. Stick to strict alternate picking (down, up) and use the finger-per-fret technique.

Example 10a –

Now double pick every note in the A Blues scale.

Example 10b –

Triple pick each note of the A Blues scale using a triplet rhythm. Listen to the accompanying audio track to hear how to play this rhythm.

Example 10c –

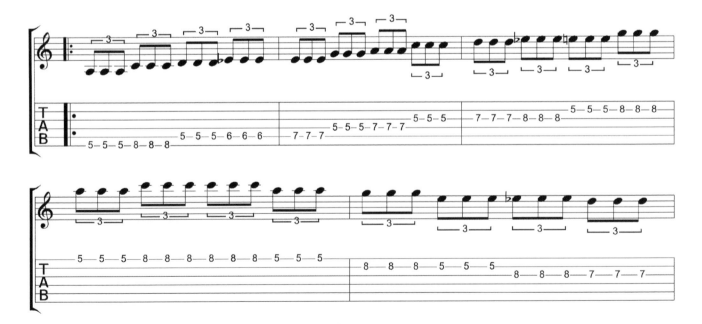

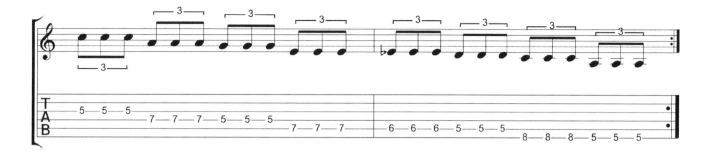

Play each of the notes of the A Blues scale four times in example 10d.

Example 10d –

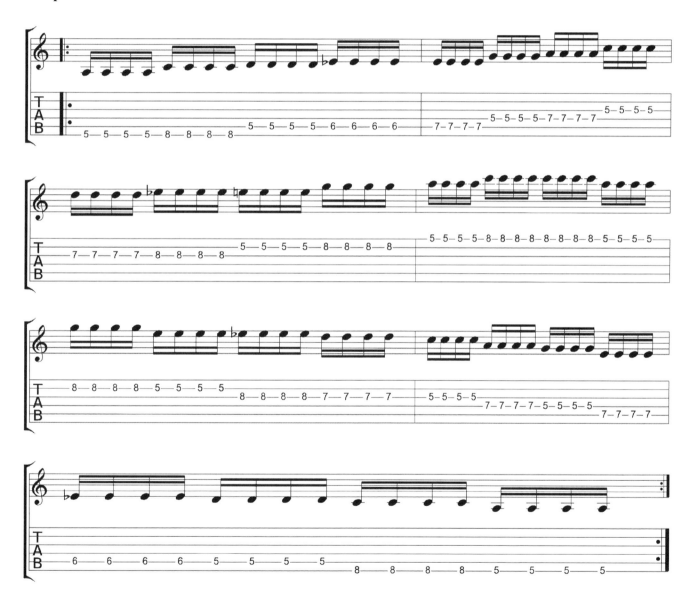

Play through the A Blues scale starting on the higher frets on each string.

Example 10e –

Work your way back through the A Blues scale shape but start from the lower fret on each string.

Example 10f –

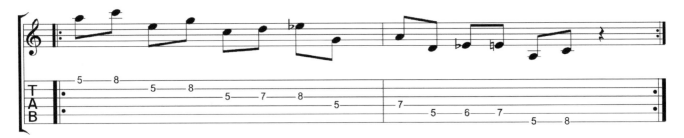

The next two examples introduce a string-skip within the A Blues scale shape. This helps you to add interesting musical jumps into your practice regime.

Example 10g –

Example 10h –

Another way to practice this scale is to combine groups of notes into patterns. Play the first three notes of the A Blues scale, then start on the second note of the scale and play the next three notes of the scale, and carry this pattern on throughout the whole shape.

Example 10i –

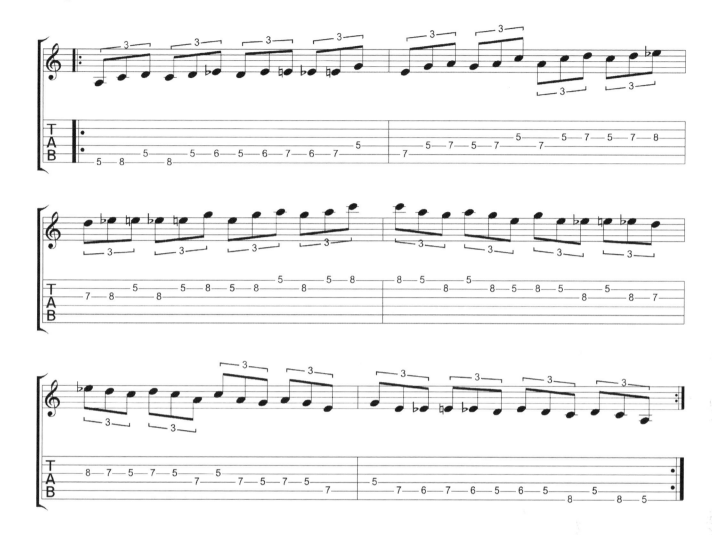

The final example in this chapter groups the A Blues scale into a pattern of four notes.

Example 10j –

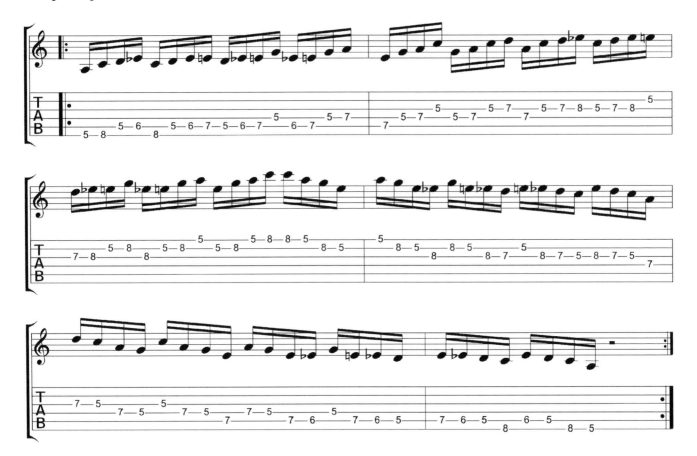

Don't rush into playing the A Blues scale licks and the full solo featured in the next two chapters before you have mastered all the examples featured in this chapter.

Practice these scale shapes with a metronome very slowly (at around 50 beats per minute) and only raise the tempo when you can play an example three times in a row. For a more musical application, play each example along with backing tracks one to four.

Pop Quiz

What notes are in the A Blues scale?

How many extra notes does the Blues scale contain than the Minor Pentatonic scale?

Name two famous guitarists that play the Blues scale.

Name three different ways you can practice playing a scale shape.

Answers on page **105**

Chapter Eleven – A Blues Scale Licks

Backing Tracks One to Four.

Now you have completed the A Blues scale technical exercises, it is time to learn some useful lick vocabulary built around this scale.

In this chapter, I have written ten A Blues scale licks based on the techniques seen throughout this book. These licks will include slides, bends and legato, so make sure you are confident with all those techniques before continuing.

The A Blues scale has one extra note than the A Minor Pentatonic scale; the note of Eb. I have made sure to focus on the Eb throughout these licks so you can get used to the unique sound of this brilliant scale.

In example 11a play the slide using your third finger. This will put your fingers in the right place for the rest of the lick.

Example 11a –

The third finger is used for all the slides featured in example 11b. Notice how bars one and three are the same, but bars two and four are different to create a 'call and response' blues lick.

Example 11b –

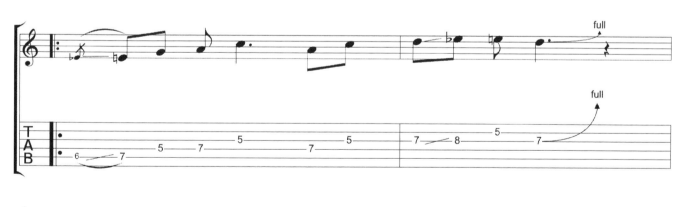

Use Backing Track Two, and start to build longer solo phrases by combining the licks featured in this chapter.

Example 11c –

Example 11d could act as a 'hook' or theme to a song or a solo because it is memorable and easy to sing.

Example 11d –

The rests between the notes give example 11e it's rhythmic, *syncopated* feel. Keep to the one-finger-per-fret technique when approaching this lick as it will work on the dexterity of all your fingers.

Example 11e –

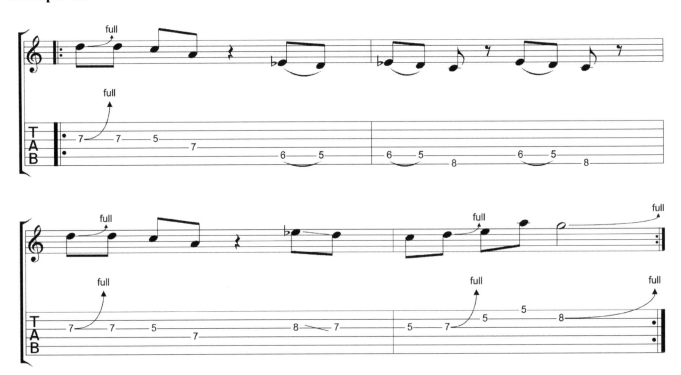

Use Backing Track Two, and start to build longer solo phrases by combining the licks featured in this chapter.

Double-stops can grab a listener's attention and sound bold and striking. This is shown in example 11f. By alternating between double-stops and single-note phrases you can add variety to your solos.

Example 11f –

Add some string-skips into your licks as demonstrated in example 11g. Musical jumps stop licks sounding sequential and scale based.

Example 11g –

Write your own lick based on the examples in this chapter. Two ways to do this are:

- Play the lick in reverse, starting from the end and working back to the beginning.
- Play the second bar before the first (or second half of the lick before the first half).

Example 11h –

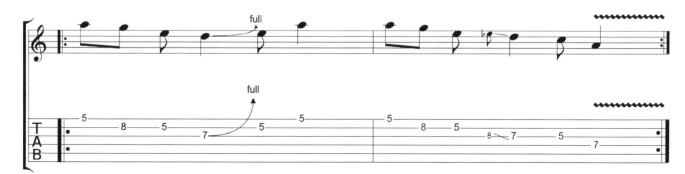

The triplet rhythm seen in example 11i acts as the focal point to the lick. Count triplets using a three-syllable word such as el-e-phant. Triplets often give a bluesy feel to a lick, so keep that in mind when writing your own material.

Example 11i –

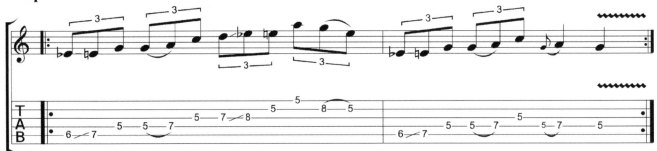

Remember that having one lick memorised is more useful than *reading* ten licks from a book. There is absolutely no rush to complete the material here, so take your time and internalise as much as possible. Most importantly enjoy making music with it!

Example 11j –

Play and use these licks as much as possible in as many different settings as you can. Play them with a metronome, play them with the backing tracks provided with this book, jam with a friend and play them with songs that are in the key of A minor. Check out the list below for some good jam songs in this key.

Songs in the Key of A Minor

- Led Zeppelin - Stairway to Heaven
- The Beatles – While My Guitar Gently Weeps
- Red Hot Chili Peppers – Californication
- U2 – Electrical Storm
- Chick – Le Freak
- Lionel Ritchie - Hello
- Maroon 5 – Secret
- Bruno Mars – When I Was Your Man

Chapter Twelve – A Blues Scale Solo

Backing Track Three

Example 12a is a full solo that uses the A Blues scale and should be played over Backing Track Three.

This is my solo favourite in this book, and the Blues scale is my favourite lead playing tool.

As with all the other full solos, listen through to the track at least three times with headphones on before playing it. You can learn this solo in its entirety or pick out specific licks that appeal to you. Either way, make sure you play along with Backing Track Three, or even better jam with a musical friend!

As well as audio of my performance on this track, I have included a slowed down midi version so you can play along at a slower tempo. **Example 12a –**

Now you have learnt the full A Blues scale solo, steal some of your favourite licks and play them over the songs mentioned at the end of the previous chapter.

When I first learnt to solo, I didn't have a teacher and I only knew the Minor Pentatonic and Blues scale shapes. I would play on every CD that my parents owned and figure out how to get my licks to work over as many different genres as possible. From Mozart to Michael Jackson, Bach to the Beatles, I spent time developing my lick vocabulary while using my ear as my guide.

Challenge

Setup a playlist with all the songs featured at the bottom of **page 73**. Press play and don't stop soloing using your A Blues licks until the final song has finished playing. Aim to vary your licks based on the genre and rhythm of the song you are playing, and repeat this exercise every day until it feels natural.

Once you feel comfortable playing along to these songs, record yourself. Even if it is just using a voice memo on your smartphone, this will serve as a good reference point for you to look back to later. Give it a title and a date for ease of reference.

Chapter Thirteen – The A Major Pentatonic Scale

The Major Pentatonic scale sounds happier than its minor counterpart and is synonymous with country, blues and rock, although it is very versatile and used in most genres. Slash, Chuck Berry and Eric Clapton are all associated with the Major Pentatonic sound.

The A Major Pentatonic contains the notes **A B C# E F#.**

The examples in this chapter will help you gain dexterity as well as fretboard fluency within the A Major Pentatonic scale.

You can play The A Major Pentatonic scale in the following way on the guitar:

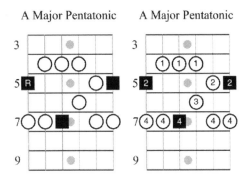

Play through the full A Major Pentatonic scale shape ascending and descending using alternate picking. Start the scale with your second finger so that you can follow the one-finger-per-fret rule. The second diagram above shows you the correct finger placements.

Example 13a –

Double pick every note of the A Major Pentatonic scale in example 13b.

Example 13b –

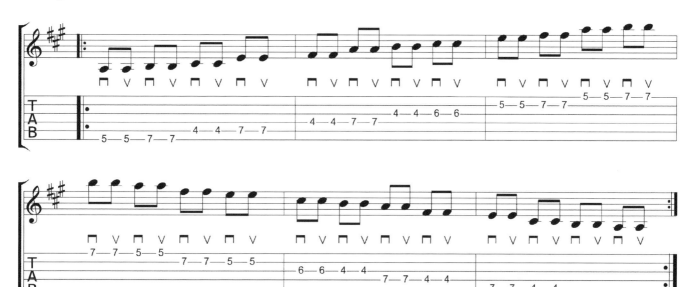

Example 13c demonstrates playing each note of the A Major Pentatonic scale three times using a triplet rhythm. Remember that you can use any three-syllable word to help you count a triplet, I prefer el-e-phant.

Example 13c –

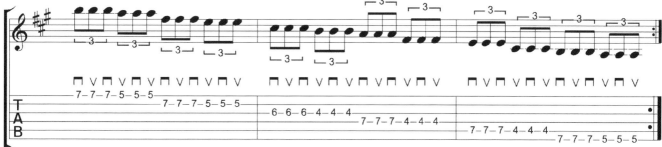

Now pick every note of the A Major Pentatonic scale four times.

Example 13d –

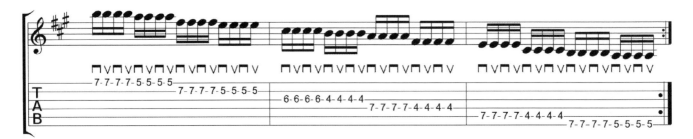

Start on the higher fret of each string and ascend through the A Major Pentatonic scale.

Example 13e –

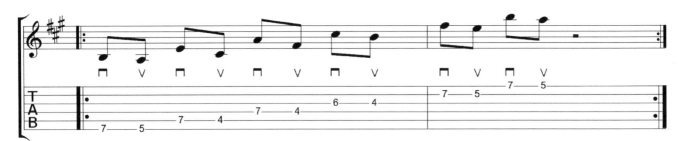

Descend through the A Major Pentatonic scale starting on the lower fret on each string.

Example 13f –

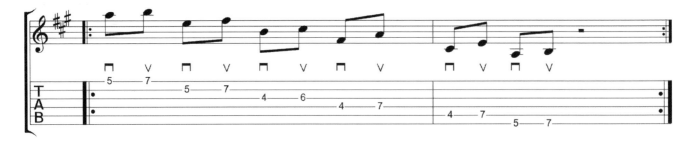

Example 13g shows how to ascend the A Major Pentatonic scale using string-skips.

Example 13g –

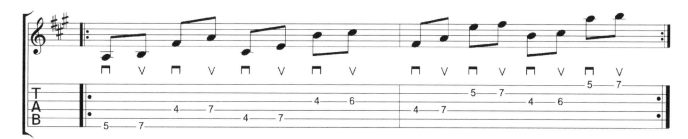

Now descend the A Major Pentatonic scale using string-skips.

Example 13h –

The next examples combine the A Major Pentatonic scale into groups of three-, four-, and six-note patterns. Practice these slowly and build up your muscle memory as these serve as great 'lick builders'!

Example 13i –

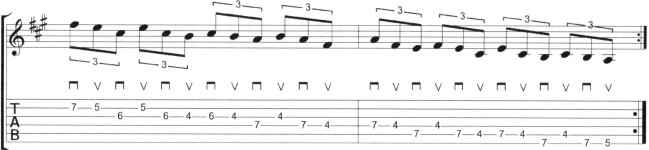

Example 13j –

Example 13k –

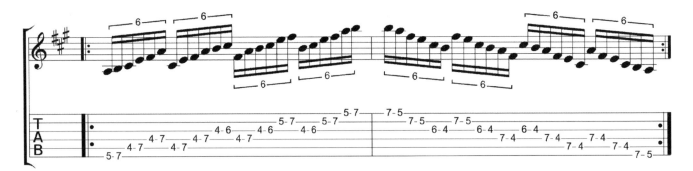

The final example in this chapter uses a 'skip-a-note' pattern. This is a useful exercise to help you break the habit of playing all the notes of the A Major Pentatonic sequentially.

Example 13l –

Pop Quiz

What are the notes in the A Major Pentatonic scale?

Name three guitarists who use the Major Pentatonic scale.

What genres of music is the Major Pentatonic scale synonymous?

How does the Major Pentatonic scale vary in sound from its Minor Pentatonic counterpart?

Answers on page **105**

Chapter Fourteen – A Major Pentatonic Licks

Backing Track Nine.

In this chapter, I have written five A Major Pentatonic scale licks that can be played with Backing Track Nine.

Be sure to practice these licks with a metronome and the backing tracks provided. Jam with a friend or solo along to the songs mentioned at the end of this chapter. Take time to internalise the licks and enjoy making your own solos from them.

The Major Pentatonic sound has a happier sound than its minor counterpart. In example 14a I have built a five-bar melodic solo around Backing Track 9 which has an expressive, vocal quality. Experiment with which finger feels most comfortable to perform the slides.

Example 14a –

Hammer-ons and pull-offs provide the backbone for this free flowing A Major Pentatonic lick. Listen to the audio and emulate how I phrase this example.

Example 14b –

In example 14c, I demonstrate how to use long swooping slow bends using the A Major Pentatonic scale. The notation gives you a visual representation of each bend that I am playing.

Example 14c –

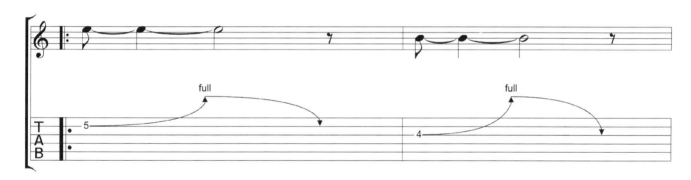

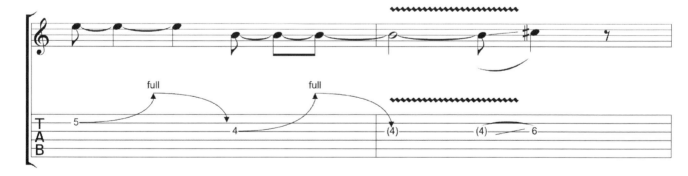

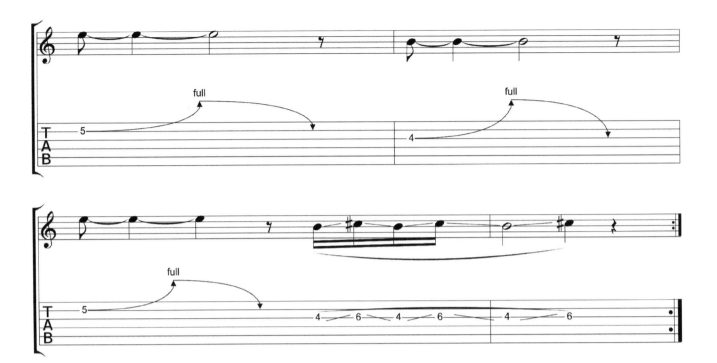

Simplicity can make for the most memorable lead guitar licks. Aim to let the hammer-on ring out while playing the note that follows.

Example 14d –

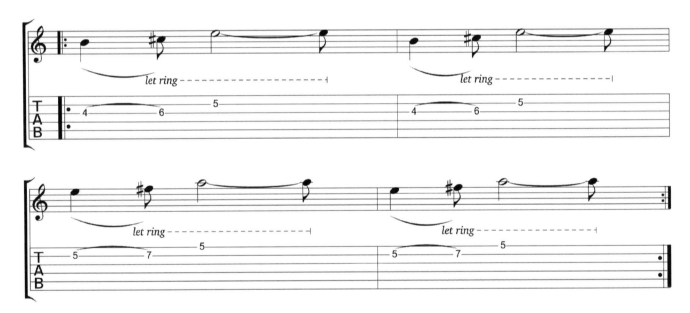

Jimi Hendrix loved to use the Major Pentatonic scale when improvising and playing solos. Check out the solo on the track The Wind Cries Mary for classic Major Pentatonic licks. Example 14e has a very Hendrix-style theme. Play the original double-stop pattern using your first finger and the second double-stop pattern using your first and second fingers.

Example 14e –

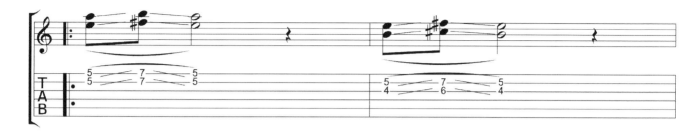

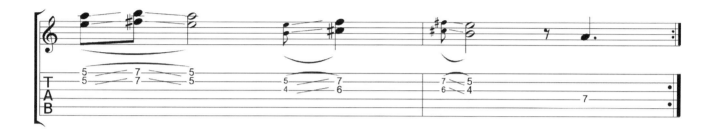

Songs in the Key of A Major

Jam along to these tunes using the licks given in this chapter.

Free – All Right Now
Eric Clapton – Tears in Heaven
The Beatles – Get Back
The Troggs – Wild Thing
Snow Patrol – Chasing Cars

Chapter Fifteen – A Major Pentatonic Solo

Backing Track Nine

Example 15a is a full solo that uses the A Major Pentatonic scale and should be played over the top of backing track nine.

Bars 9 – 14 will need to be practiced at a slower speed before bringing them up to speed. I have included the picking directions above each note of this section to tell you precisely how I approach playing this lick. This section has a classic rock sound and is similar to the end of the Free track, All Right Now.

All of the licks for the Major Pentatonic scale in this book are presented in the key of A, but it is crucially important that you spend time moving these licks and ideas around the fretboard to all twelve keys. Refer to **page 59** for how to find the root notes on the 6th string.

As always, I have included a slowed down midi version so you can play along at a slower tempo.

Example 15a –

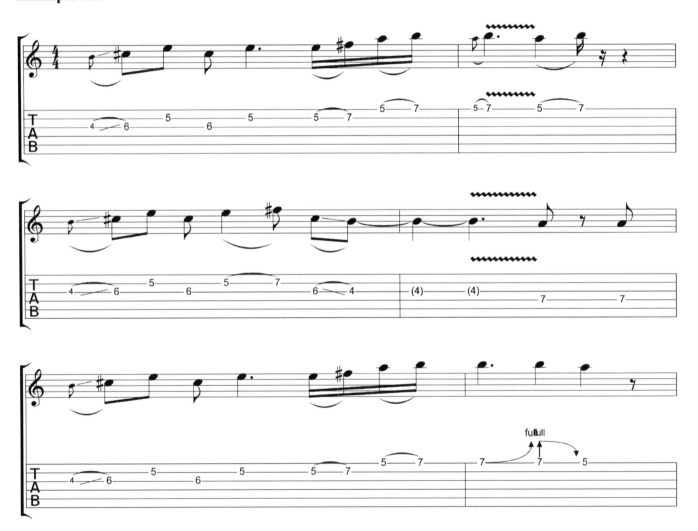

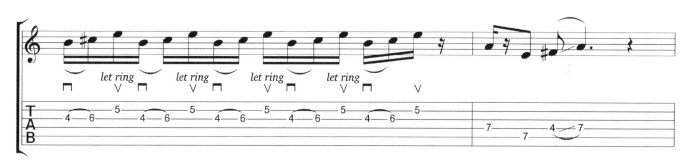

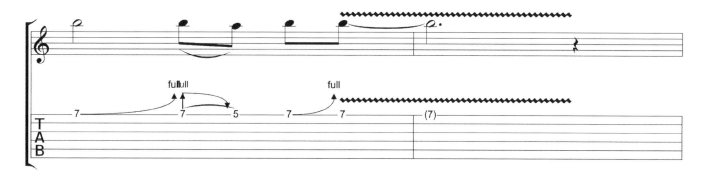

Buy A Looper Pedal

One of the most useful tools I have ever bought in my guitar playing career is a looper pedal. It is the perfect jam companion and will always be the same level as you! I personally use a Ditto looper pedal in my practice regimes and lessons as I can quickly lay down a rhythmic idea or just a chord and then solo over it.

Alternatively, you can use the voice memo function on your smartphone to record a loop, and use that as your backing track.

Chapter Sixteen – The Four Note Soloing Challenge

Backing Track Three

Watch my Bonus Content Video Lesson for this chapter here:

www.fundamental-changes.com/ssbc

Although the scale shapes you have learnt should now feel comfortable to you, it can still seem daunting to create your own licks and solos with them. Enter the four-note soloing challenge!

The principal behind this challenge is simple: Pick a scale shape you know well, and restrict yourself to playing *only* four notes from that scale.

In example 16a, I have created a full solo based on just four notes of the A Minor Pentatonic scale. Shown below are the notes I have used to create this full solo.

A Minor Pentatonic

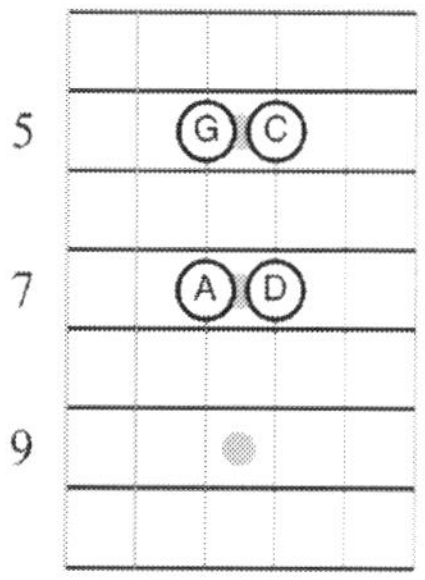

At first, the possibilities seem incredibly limited when dealing with just these four notes, but by applying bends, hammer-ons, pull-offs, slides and vibrato, the number of melodic options is vast.

Learn and study the solo I have created here before attempting to create your own solo using this four-note system. Steal as many licks as you can from this solo, and from all the earlier chapters based around the A Minor Pentatonic scale too.

Example 16a -

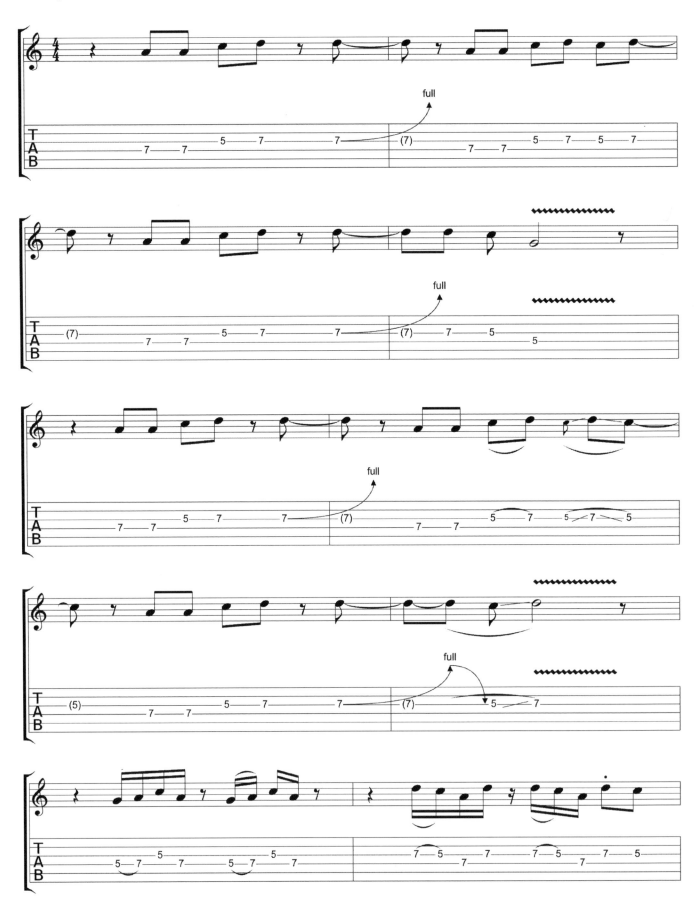

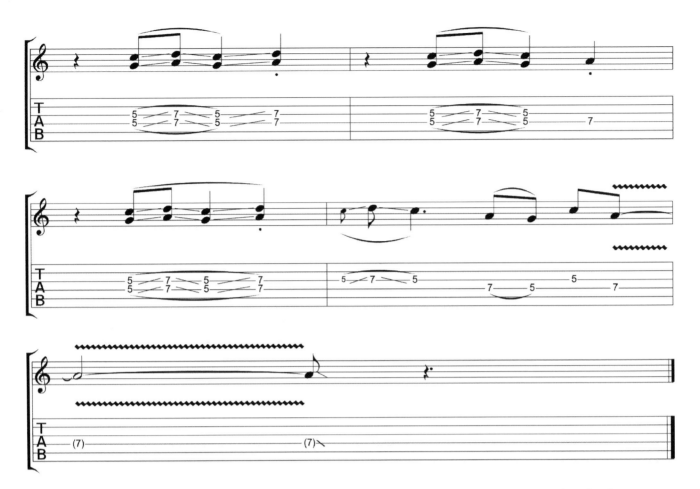

Once you have completed example 16a and feel comfortable creating your own solos using the four notes, you can apply this same strategy to *any* four notes from *any* scale shape.

For starters create a solo over backing track one using just these four notes from the highest part of the A Minor Pentatonic scale.

A Minor Pentatonic

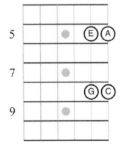

After you have completed the four note challenges with the A Minor Pentatonic scale, apply this idea to the E Minor Pentatonic scale, the A Blues scale and the A Major scale.

If you have created your own solo using this four-note soloing strategy, record a video of yourself playing and post it as a comment underneath the YouTube video featured at the start of this chapter.

Chapter Seventeen – 'In The Style of' Licks

Backing Track Five and Six

Jimi Hendrix, Eric Clapton, B.B. King, Stevie Ray Vaughan and David Gilmour are undisputable guitar legends. I have created five 'in the style of' licks in the key of E Minor, one for each of these artists.

Hendrix redefined electric guitar playing and changed the course of modern day soloing. Example 17a combines ideas from tracks like Hey Joe and Little Wing to form a blues-rock Hendrix-style lead line suitable for any backing track in the key of E Minor. As always, make sure you move all these licks to as many different keys as possible.

Example 17a – Hendrix

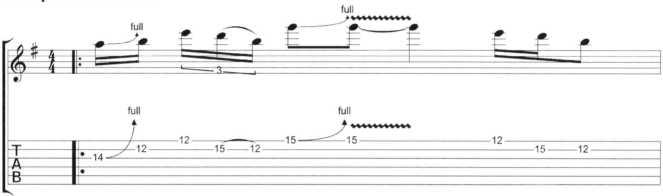

Triplets provide the basis for this blues-based E minor Eric Clapton style lick. Notice the combination of double-stops and single notes in this four-bar idea. I recommend checking out the lesser known track My Father's Eyes for a passionate Clapton song that's full of emotion.

Example 17b – Eric Clapton

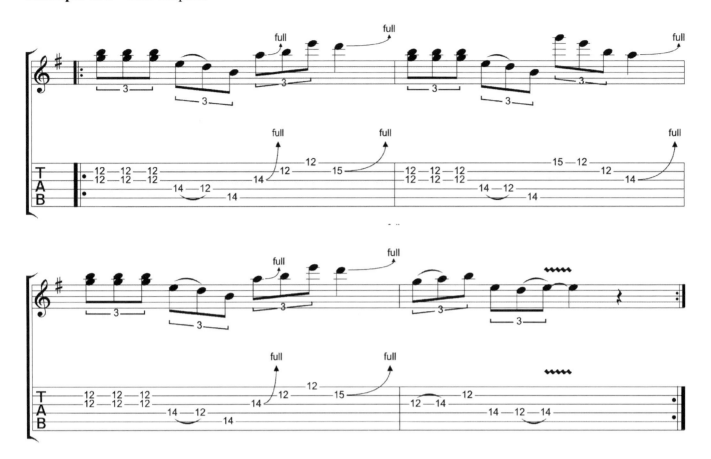

B.B. King could make just one note sing! His style is instantly recognisable; from his trademark vibrato to the beautiful touch, tone and expression in everything he played. Check out the classic track The Thrill is Gone for more licks in this style.

Example 17c – B.B. King

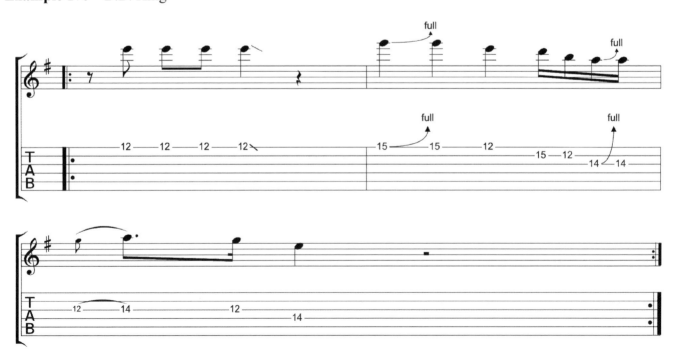

Stevie Ray Vaughan was of the most passionate players ever, combining his raw Texas Blues background with speed and prowess everywhere on the neck. Listen to the huge hit Texas Flood for more tasty SRV licks.

Example 17d – Stevie Ray Vaughan

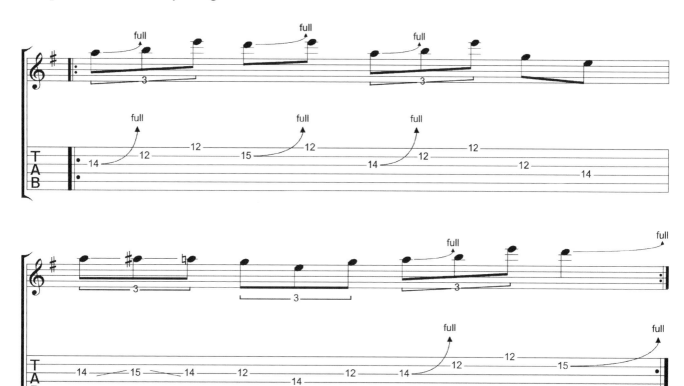

Famed for his time with Pink Floyd, David Gilmour is synonymous with the finest blues guitar licks around combining silky-smooth lead guitar and a classic Fender Stratocaster sound.

Example 17e – David Gilmour

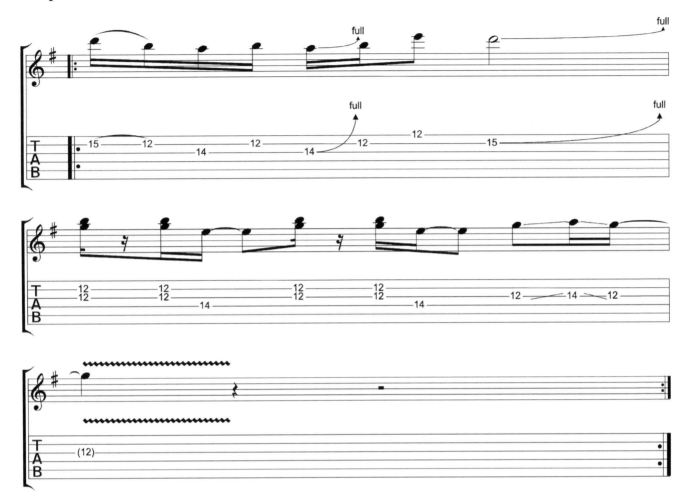

There is something incredibly satisfying about learning to play licks in the style of your guitar heroes and I have written a wide and varied selection of video articles based around guitar giants and how to play in their style.

Check out the **Fundamental Changes YouTube** channel for lots of free videos to push you to the next level in your guitar playing. **http://www.youtube.com/c/FundamentalchangesGuitar**

Sample Practice Workouts

The perfect lead guitar workout is one that fits around your individual needs, interests and ability. I have created ten-minute, fifteen-minute, thirty-minute and one-hour workout suggestions for you below. These workouts are a guide and can be customised in any way you wish.

Use a metronome and a timer for each workout.

Sample 10 Minute Workout

Example Number	Metronome Speed	Total Time
1b	50bpm (Increase Daily)	1 Minute
1l	50bpm (Increase Daily)	1 Minute
2i	50bpm (Increase Daily)	1 Minute
2k	50bpm (Increase Daily)	1 Minute
3o	50bpm (Increase Daily)	1 Minute
4w	50bpm (Increase Daily)	1 Minute
5z	50bpm (Increase Daily)	1 Minute
6c	50bpm (Increase Daily)	1 Minute
7a	50bpm (Increase Daily)	2 Minutes
		10 Minutes

Sample 15 Minute Workout

Example Number	Metronome Speed	Total Time
1i	50bpm (Increase Daily)	1 Minute
1l	50bpm (Increase Daily)	1 Minute
2j	50bpm (Increase Daily)	1 Minute
3e	50bpm (Increase Daily)	1 Minute
3n	50bpm (Increase Daily)	1 Minute
4x	50bpm (Increase Daily)	1 Minute
5zc	50bpm (Increase Daily)	1 Minute
6f	50bpm (Increase Daily)	1 Minute
7a	50bpm (Increase Daily)	3 Minutes
8b	50bpm (Increase Daily)	1 Minute
9a	50bpm (Increase Daily)	3 Minutes
		15 Minutes

Sample 30 Minute Workout

You can now spend longer on each example, giving you more time to practice any patterns or sequences you find challenging.

Example Number	Metronome Speed	Total Time
1d	50bpm (Increase Daily)	2 Minutes
2k	50bpm (Increase Daily)	2 Minutes
3o	50bpm (Increase Daily)	2 Minutes
4g	50bpm (Increase Daily)	2 Minutes
5z2	50bpm (Increase Daily)	2 Minutes
6h	50bpm (Increase Daily)	2 Minutes
7a	50bpm (Increase Daily)	3 Minutes
8i	50bpm (Increase Daily)	2 Minutes
9a	50bpm (Increase Daily)	3 Minutes
12a	50bpm (Increase Daily)	3 Minutes
15a	50bpm (Increase Daily)	3 Minutes
16a	50bpm (Increase Daily)	4 Minutes
		30 Minutes

Sample 60 Minute Workout

Example Number	Metronome Speed	Total Time
1e	50bpm (Increase Daily)	2 Minutes
2o	50bpm (Increase Daily)	3 Minutes
3o	50bpm (Increase Daily)	3 Minutes
4z	50bpm (Increase Daily)	3 Minutes
5z5	50bpm (Increase Daily)	3 Minutes
6d	50bpm (Increase Daily)	3 Minutes
7a	50bpm (Increase Daily)	5 Minutes
8d	50bpm (Increase Daily)	3 Minutes
9a	50bpm (Increase Daily)	5 Minutes
12a	50bpm (Increase Daily)	5 Minutes
13b	50bpm (Increase Daily)	5 Minutes
14a	50bpm (Increase Daily)	5 Minutes
15a	50bpm (Increase Daily)	5 Minutes
16a	50bpm (Increase Daily)	5 Minutes
17c	50bpm (Increase Daily)	5 Minutes
		60 Minutes

Conclusion

By now, you are probably swimming in a sea of new ideas and possibilities. I recommend you create your own personal video lick diary for reference. Film your licks, and if possible write them out in standard notation or tab. That way, when you look back in six months' time, not only can you see and hear how far your playing has come, you can revisit licks that you may have forgotten.

Practice what you don't know, not what you do! - This is quite simply the best advice I can give any musician. Use a metronome to help you master each example and use backing tracks to create a more musical approach to practicing.

An important goal should be to play with other people, so while you are developing your skills in this book find time to jam with other musicians. Playing with other instrumentalists is the best way to improve your musicianship.

Be sure to check out my other titles also released on the Fundamental Changes label:

My passion in life is teaching people to play and express themselves through the guitar. If you have any questions, please get in touch and I will do my best to respond as quickly as possible.

You can contact me on **simeypratt@gmail.com** or via the **Fundamental Changes YouTube channel**.

Discography

Here are some classic songs that contain either amazing solos or incredible lead guitar work throughout.

Albert King – Born Under a Bad Sign
Eric Clapton – Crossroads
Jimi Hendrix – All Along the Watchtower / Little Wing
B.B King – The Thrill is Gone
Leslie West – Mississippi Queen
Richie Blackmore – Highway Star (Deep Purple)
Billy Gibbons – La Grange (ZZ Top)
Larry Carlton – Kid Charlemagne
Carlos Santana – Samba Pa Ti
Eddie Van Halen – Eruption
Mark Knopfler – Sultans of Swing (Dire Straights)
Michael Schenker – Rock Bottom
David Gilmour – Another Brick in The Wall PT 2
Angus Young – You Shook Me All Night Long
Randy Rhoads – Crazy Train
Stevie Ray Vaughan – Pride and Joy
Yngwie Malmsteen – Black Star
Kirk Hammett – Master of Puppets
Joe Satriani – Always With Me, Always With You
Kurt Cobain – Come as You Are
Zakk Wylde – No More Tears
Dimebag Darrell – Cowboys from Hell
Slash – November Rain
Steve Vai – For The Love of God
The Scorpions – Rock You Like a Hurricane
The Surfaris – Wipeout
The Beatles – Something
Lynyrd Skynyrd – Sweet Home Alabama
Allman Brothers Band – Stormy Monday / Jessica
Toto – Rossana
Rush – Limelight
Tower of Power
The Doobie Brothers – China Groove
Ram Jam – Black Betty
Gary Moore – Parisian Walkways
Eric Johnson – Cliffs of Dover
Yngwie Malmsteen – Rising Force
Steve Vai – For The Love of God
Joe Satriani – Cryin'

Quiz Answers

P19

- A C D E G
- Melodic building blocks can act as the stepping stone to creating longer licks and eventually solos.

P24

- There are two types of slide, an upward and a downward.
- An upward slide is from a lower pitch to a higher one.
- A double slide is sliding between multiple notes using only one pick stroke
- Blues, Rock, Country, Jazz and Funk.

P34

- Bending is the technique of raising the pitch of a note by increasing the tension on the string.
- A semi-tone bend raises the pitch of a note by a half-step, or one fret.
- A tone bend raises the pitch of a note by a whole-step, or two frets.
- A tone bend is the most common in modern day electric guitar playing.
- David Gilmour, Jimi Hendrix and Carlos Santana.

P64

- E G A B D.
- Two notes played at the same time.
- Repeat certain licks throughout a solo.
- At least three times.

P70

- A C D Eb E G.
- One – the note of Eb.
- Angus Young and Joe Satriani.
- Multiple picks on every note, skip a string and groupings of notes.

P83

- A B C# E F#.
- Slash, Chuck Berry and Eric Clapton.
- Country, blues and rock.
- The Major Pentatonic scale sounds happier than its minor counterpart.

Other Books from Fundamental Changes

43742918R00061

Made in the USA
San Bernardino, CA
26 December 2016